Stories from
INDIA

VOLUME TWO

WISDOM STORIES *series*

"Timeless Tales Told by Paramhansa Yogananda"

Stories from India, Volume One
Stories from India, Volume Two

Stories from
INDIA

VOLUME TWO

Paramhansa Yogananda

CRYSTAL CLARITY PUBLISHERS   Commerce, California

CRYSTAL CLARITY PUBLISHERS
1123 Goodrich Blvd. | Commerce, California
crystalclarity.com | 800.424.1055
clarity@crystalclarity.com

ISBN 978-1-56589-115-9 (print)
ISBN 978-1-56589-637-6 (e-book)
Library of Congress Cataloging-in-Publication Data
   2022053588 (print) | 2022053589 (e-book)

Compiled and edited by Nayaswami Maria
Cover and interior design and layout by Michele Madhavi Molloy

The *Joy Is Within You* symbol is registered by Ananda Church
of Self-Realization of Nevada County, California.

Dedicated to all children of the Divine Mother

Contents

Wisdom

Indices

With unceasing blessing,
Paramhansa Yogananda.

Introduction

he research for Stories from India by Paramhansa Yogananda unearthed many wonderful tales that continue to inspire, offer deep insights, and overall, entertain our hearts and lives. It is our joy to offer to you this second volume.

Stories are a powerful teacher. They enter into our consciousness, captivating our imagination with characters and fantastic story lines. Beneath the surface, they reveal the age-old drama of humankind with circumstances and plots not so very different from the times we live in today. Certainly parallels, and more importantly lessons, can be drawn that continue to teach and change the way we live, the way we relate to one another.

I have met many people from around the world, reared on traditional stories unique to their culture. These stories have imparted lifelong traits of compassion and understanding, virtue, *dharma* (right action), the ability to relate to another's reality. As a universal medium they reach into the hearts of all God's children — young and old — delivering timeless truths in ways easy to digest and assimilate. Perhaps, more than anything, this is why Paramhansa Yogananda enjoyed sharing stories and why his direct disciple, Swami Kriyananda, did the same through his lectures, *satsangs* and many books. Such stories allowed people to relax, be fully present and receptive, and understand truths and subtleties they might otherwise have missed. Certainly these stories opened doors of understanding and continue to do so.

For your pleasure and reference, we have cataloged these stories according to their predominant spiritual quality in addition to the typical Table of Contents by title.

It is our hope that you enjoy these stories, take the time to be with them, and share them with your friends in the company of the master storyteller himself, Paramhansa Yogananda, in your own heart.

Boundless Blessings,
Nayaswami Maria

Stories from
INDIA

VOLUME TWO

Humility

The Most Humble God

Ages ago, Saint Bhrigu of India had
a desire to find the most humble form God had
ever taken. He wandered all over the Himalayan
Mountains and the holy places in search of some
incarnation of God he could accept as a guru. But,
since he wished an example of humility to follow,
he determined that the God must have this attri-
bute. He met many Saints, whom he questioned
as to where he could find such a god-guru. After
a strenuous search, he found that all the Saints
that he met gave him the names of the same three
forms of God, Brahma, Shiva, and Vishnu, who
was then incarnated as Krishna — and assured
him that one of them was sure to be the right one.

Saint Bhrigu heard that Brahma could create
anything, Shiva could destroy anything, and Krishna
(Vishnu) could preserve anything from annihilation,
for they represented the creative, destructive, and
preservative principles active in all Creation.

Bewildered as to who was the humblest and greatest of the three, he conceived a queer plan to test them. His great powers, gained through meditation, enabled him to leave his body and find God, in the form of Brahma, on the astral plane. Without much ceremony of introduction, in a very disrespectful manner he began to criticize him. "Hey, Brahma, what is the matter with you? Why don't you stand up and greet me when I come?"

Brahma inwardly was astonished at the audacity of this mortal man and retorted: "Do you know to whom you are talking?" "Yes sir," said Bhrigu, "of course, I know that I am talking to that despicable God who is the creator of vermin, plagues, mosquitoes, diseases, criminals, and all ugly things in Creation. Why don't you reform *yourself* and create only good things?" Brahma was beside himself with wrath and threateningly replied: "Get back to earth before I convert you into a stone by the gorgon gaze of my will."

Saint Bhrigu laughed at him and left, saying: "O no, you cannot hate me or make me into a stone, for God and I are One." Brahma suddenly awoke from his error and apologized. Then Bhrigu said: "I forgive you Brahma, but I am disappointed not to have found in you what I wanted to see."

Then Bhrigu repaired to Shiva, who was seen getting ready to meditate on all the things beyond their prime that must be brought to an end. As soon as Shiva's form met the gaze of Bhrigu, the

Saint shouted savagely: "Hey, Shiva, you Grand Cosmic Killer, why don't you stop shattering worlds, murdering innocent babies, and inventing ingenious death-dealing devices? Why don't you cease destroying the beautiful and useful things and beings of the earth and get busy annihilating the wicked things?"

Shiva could not believe his ears, that a mortal man like Saint Bhrigu could be so audacious and free with his speech. He shouted: "Shut up, or I will reduce you to ashes with the burning magnetism of my Spiritual Eye." Saint Bhrigu derisively retorted: "Fine use you will make of your Spiritual Eye. Go ahead, I dare you to burn up the God in me, you Grand Killer!" Shiva remained paralyzed with anger and speechless at the awakening words of Saint Bhrigu, who soon melted away from his sight, saying: "Oh, what a disappointment you are."

At last, almost despairing because he could not find the world's most humble God, he skeptically resorted to the third God — Vishnu, who controlled the preserving principle of the Cosmos. But this time he stayed on earth and sought out the prophet Krishna — in whom these great powers were manifesting. Saint Bhrigu found Prophet Krishna sound asleep on a sofa in his palace. He stood there watching the halo of peace radiating from the prophetic face of Krishna. Then, unable to think of any way to test him, in a fit of emotion Saint Bhrigu kicked Krishna on the chest, shouting: "You sleeping fool, wake up, see who is here." Krishna awakened with the sweetest, most undismayed, loving smile, and quickly picked up the kicking foot of Saint Bhrigu, and while massaging it, he said gently: "Ah, my Lord Bhrigu, is your foot hurt?"

Saint Bhrigu, beside himself with simultaneous visitations of remorse and joy, cried out: "I have found him. I have found him. O, Prophet Krishna, Thou art the world's most humble Being, even as God is. Thou art, O Krishna, the greatest, the most humble form of God. *You* can teach me. I accept you as my Guru. Will you accept me?" And Krishna accepted Bhrigu as his disciple.

Wisdom Gem

Now, DEAR FRIENDS, you realize that if you want to know the greatest of all Beings, the wisest in the Cosmos, our God, you must be humble, for the humble man makes a charming altar for God in himself, and establishes his altar of humility in every heart that he meets.

— by Paramhansa Yogananda

The Three Gods and The Lord of Gods

s a wave springs from the breast of the sea, plays around o'er its blue tracts for a while, and, when tired, falls asleep again on its lap, so also, Creation, with its dolls of Universes, is born out of the matrix of space, and plays the Cosmic planetary game until tired, and then falls asleep in the chamber of the living Void.

It is said that the storm creates a wave, preserves its shape, and then ultimately dissolves it in the sea-breast. It would be quite audacious for the waves to think that they create themselves, preserve themselves, and dissolve themselves again without the aid of any force.

There is an old story that three intelligent Beings emanated from God, namely, Brahma, the creator of all things, Vishnu, the preserver of all things, and Shiva, the destroyer of all things. All waves of Creation were lifted by Brahma;

they were sustained by Vishnu, and were dissolved by Shiva.

Once upon a time these three omnipresent gods materialized themselves into the forms of human beings in order to visit the old earth — the playground of their activities. These three gods roamed upon the earth, beholding vast empires and multitudes of people, and watched their birth, preservation, and death. The triad of deities, beholding their own colossal works, fell into a state of self-laudation and entered into a discussion of their mutual powers. Brahma said: "Friends, look at the stars, suns, moons, worlds, inhabitants, vegetation, and the wise Souls that I have created." Vishnu couldn't keep quiet any longer after hearing his friend's self-praise and cried out: "Friends, behold the power of my preservation. All things were created all right, but unless I held them balanced with the strings of my self-emanated rays, the worlds would collide and perish and men would perish without food." Then Shiva impatiently cried: "Friends, behold, I am powerful enough to dissolve all your created and preserved Creations."

The three gods came to the middle of a beautiful field, sat down, and in unison cried out: "Aren't we wonderful? We are the supreme gods — the creator, preserver, and destroyer." And then Brahma said: "It is I, the matchless one, who creates all the beauties in Nature." Vishnu cried: "But it is I who give the lease of life to all your beautiful things."

And Shiva cried: "And it is I who destroy the monotony, the sameness of everything by dissolving them into the furnace of my Being and renewing them into something different for you, Brahma, to create and mold." And again the three gods chorused in unison: "Aren't we wonderful?"

Even as this merriment was going on, a little child with night-dark eyes suddenly sprang out of the ether and stood in front of Brahma and asked: "Who are you?" Laughingly Brahma replied: "Why, don't you know? I am the creator of all things." The little child laughed and saucily replied "Well, Mr. Brahma, scratch your brain and find out if you ever created me, I was never created by you." Brahma searched the memory of his omniscience, but at last, exhausted, he sat down in despair and replied: "O little boy, you must have been created by me but I don't remember. Yet, I don't think that I created you." Then the lotus-eyed boy challenged Vishnu and asked if he were sustaining his life. "Of course, I think I sustain you, but I can't remember," replied Vishnu, who taxed his memory but was forced to admit that he had not been sustaining the audacious little boy. Then, turning to the most elated and puffed up, self-contained god, Shiva, the little boy challenged him: "Shiva, you can never kill me, no matter what you do." And Shiva, no matter how he tried, found that he could not even use his will power to seek to destroy the child.

Then the three gods asked: "Audacious little boy, whence comest thou?" But the little boy laughed and put a small piece of straw in front of the three Gods and addressed Brahma thus: "O mighty, self-appointed creator of universes, use your will and try to create, if you can, another piece of straw just like the one you see before you." Brahma floated the Cosmic Energy out of him and willed himself into a nervous wreck, but still he could not create a duplicate piece of straw. With beads of perspiration running down his cheeks, and with bowed head, the puzzled Brahma sat down vanquished and ashamed.

Then the little boy said: "Vishnu, please try to save that little piece of straw that I am going to destroy." Saying this, the little fellow belched smoke and fire through his body, threw a flame at the piece of straw and it melted and vanished. Vishnu, with all his preserving, almighty will-command, could not keep that little piece of straw from being destroyed.

Then the little boy with fiery eyes looked at the uncomfortable Shiva and spoke: "Behold, I bring back the little piece of straw." And the little straw reappeared to grace their vision. And now the little boy turned to Shiva and said: "Almighty Shiva, dissolver of all things, please try to dissolve this little piece of straw." Insulted and challenged, Shiva opened up his Spiritual Eye and let loose a flood of world-dissolving, all-melting fire. But no matter how Shiva foamed fire and set all the forest of space ablaze, still he could not even singe the piece of straw. At last the gods closed their eyes and hung their heads in shame. Then suddenly all three cried out in unison: "Shining, blessed little child, who are you?"

When the three Gods heard no response, they opened their eyes and found the little boy dissolving into the ether and gently saying: "You have yet to find out who I am — I, whose residence is in you and in everything else."

Wisdom Gem

THIS STORY ILLUSTRATES that, no matter how powerful one becomes in life, he must not forget his entire dependence upon the Cosmic Fountain of Life — the Life of all life, the God of all gods.

Pride is blinding, for it banishes the vision of vastness inhabiting greater Souls. No matter how great a person is in a certain field, there will be found in time a greater one in the same orbit of achievement. So, no matter how great you are, never forget that, lurking in the dark pathways of life, there may be someone greater than you.

As was true of the three most powerful Gods in the foregoing story, who became wiser through the knowledge that their powers were nothing but the borrowed powers of His Supreme Excellency. So, before pride blinds you and shuts out the vision of the Infinite, you must know that, no matter whether you are a successful businessman, or a powerful politician, or a dictator, or a great reformer, your power is nothing but the reflected power of God. Humbleness is the open gate through which the Divine flood of mercy and power loves to flow into recipient Souls.

— by Paramhansa Yogananda

Sustainer of the Universe

ogananda told the story about a devotee offering flowers on the altar. All of a sudden he entered cosmic consciousness. "Oh!" he cried, "I have been worshiping another's image, and now I see that I, untouched by the body, am the Sustainer of the universe: I bow to myself!" And he began throwing the flowers on his own head. He wasn't being arrogant. Nor was he denying that he had ever been a devotee. He was simply recognizing that, although for incarnations he had been sleeping in delusion, he had now awakened to his true Self. That Self, for all of us, is the Supreme Spirit.

Wisdom Gem

IN THE RETELLING of this story, Swami Kriyananda, a direct disciple of Paramhansa Yogananda, expressed the following:

The soul, after it attains Self-realization, knows that it never lived in delusion at all, for everything it experienced during all its incarnations was a dream. Thus, every awakened master is in the same position Krishna was to state: "I am birthless and eternal; never have I lived in human form." What such a master means is simply the same truth Sri Krishna himself uttered in the Bhagavad Gita, "The soul [everyone's soul, in other words] is never born; nor does it die."

I have known saints to declare, "I have never incarnated," yet on other occasions tell certain persons, "We have been together in other lives." They were not contradicting themselves. Their meaning was determined by their point of view at the moment. A master has reached that state of realization in which the soul perceives that everything is only a dream.

— by Swami Kriyananda

Faith

The Fisherman and the Hindu Priest

In ancient India, in a village on the River Ganges, lived a fisherman who used to catch and sell fish to the villagers. The village priest continuously bought fish on a charge account, and never paid what he owed to the fisherman. When the unpaid debts became very large, the fisherman, after a long siege, at last got hold of the slippery, dodging priest and accosted him thus:

"Your Holiness, why do you avoid me? Why don't you teach me a method of walking on the water, so that I can go freely to the well-known places where large schools of fish swim, and net them? I assure you that if you grant me this favor, I will present you with large fish free of charge, and I will cancel your debt to me."

The disbelieving priest, in order to get rid of the crazy fisherman, (at least the priest thought him crazy) whispered into the attentive and very faithful ears of the fisherman: "Son, all you have to do is to write on the surface of your palm the sacred word 'Om, Om, Om,' three times, and then you will be all ready to walk over the Ganges to wherever you want to catch fish."

Days passed before the fisherman could again catch the dodging priest. Then he said to the priest: "I have been trying to get hold of you in order to give you some fish and cancel your debt to me. Everything came through your grace, as you said it would."

Astonished, the skeptical priest cried: "What did you do to get such nice big fish?"

"Well sir, I did what you told me to do, and every day I have been catching a large number of fish. Yes, your Holiness, it was possible through your grace and Spiritual technique."

Half credulous and half in ridicule, the priest shouted: "Well, sirrah, show me how you walk on the water."

The fisherman caught hold of the elbow of the priest. The sacred word "Om" was thrice forcibly written on the palm of both his hands. Then casually and nonchalantly, in great Divine faith, the fisherman, holding the hand of the priest, began to walk swiftly over the water of the holy river Ganges and lo! the priest was walking over the water also. But in a little while as the skeptical priest feared drowning and began to pull up his cloak lest it get wet he began to sink and cried out: "Look fisherman! I am drowning."

"Well, your Holiness, you can't walk on the water and at the same time fear and try to save your skirts from being drenched. Look at me and see how I walk on the water with faith." Saying this, the fisherman led the trembling priest back to shore and left him to meditate on his weakness and lack of faith in God.

Wisdom Gem

JESUS SAID: "IF thou dost believe and say unto this mountain, 'go into the depths of the sea,' it shall go."

But do not expect it to obey if you go to a mountain and say with a timid, unbelieving, squeaky voice: "Mr. Mountain, will you please go in to the depths of the sea? You know I don't believe it possible, but I am only saying what Jesus said."

Miracles are nothing but the working of super-laws and they can be performed ordinarily in a common way when one is acquainted with the scientific relation between matter and mind. Jesus walked on the waters and saved the skeptical drowning Peter.

But remember, do not try to do difficult things unless you know the real method of working the miracle of faith and will power. Do not try to walk on water. Develop your faith first and try to work it to solve small difficulties. Then you will be able to open the Gordian knots of the most abstruse problems of life.

This story shows that you must know the spiritual technique as well as have absolute faith and abandonment in God if you aspire to work His miracles, and that if you are skeptical and try to perform great miracles you may be beset by severe difficulties.

— by Paramhansa Yogananda

God Alone

There's a story of a man who was a yogi and a saint, but he was married. He always used to pray, however, "God, whenever you call me I will leave in a moment." Affirming his inner freedom in this manner was his daily prayer.

After some time his wife gave birth to their first child, and in the process of giving birth she died. The little child was lying there completely helpless, no one to take care of her. Then this saint heard God call, saying to him, "My beloved, you've said that you would answer My call. Now, I call you: come to Me!" The saint said, "Lord, I believe! But how can I leave this baby?" Then, with renewed vigor, standing firm in his promise, he said, "No, Lord, I will believe You. You've called me, and I know You'll take care of this child. But at least give me the satisfaction of knowing how You'll take care of it."

The man went and hid behind a bush and was listening to the abandoned child's cries. Just then, the queen — the *maharani* — was driving by in her chariot. She heard this little baby crying and she got down and picked up the baby saying, "Oh, I am without a child. This will be my child!"

The yogi understood and he went to the Himalayas and devoted the rest of his life to his romance with the only Beloved.

Wisdom Gem

THERE *DOES* COME a time when you are so free that a life alone with God *is* your highest duty, because He is the only beloved. When you've reached that point, then He will call you and *you will know*. This kind of opportunity comes after many lives of struggle: many lives of effort and meditation.

Important to note is the heartfelt willingness of the devotee to think of God in whatever He has given you to do in life and to offer all your efforts to God Alone.

— by Nayaswami Maria

Right Action
(Dharma)

The Reward of Virtue

n Hindustan, once upon a time, there lived a very spiritual-minded King, who was beloved by his subjects as much for his great liberality to all as for his just and impartial rule. He was also very fond of holy men and delighted in their company. He always showered his choicest gifts upon them.

One day a scheming rascal, who pretended to be a holy man, came to the King and said to him: "O Prince, I have lived the life of a recluse, only now and then stirring out into the great world to visit ancient shrines and places of pilgrimage by the sacred rivers. I feel extremely curious to know what a three-days' change in my dull, joyless, ascetic life would feel like. So do thou, O Prince, let me rule over thy kingdom just for three days in thy place." The King, who never denied anything to a holy man, agreed to this, so with his Queen and his two little sons he left his State on a three-days' holiday.

The "holy" man now took off his yellow robe and put on the gorgeous dress of a Prince. He sat on the throne with a golden crown on his head and a jeweled scepter in his hand, and thus began his three days' reign.

When the three-days' rule was over, the King returned to claim his Kingdom, but the "holy" man, loath to part with the scepter so soon, said to the King: "O generous Prince! I have tasted the sweets of power, but my three days' rule has expired too soon. Let me continue to reign over thy Kingdom just a little longer."

"A holy man," thought the King, "knows the Scriptures, so he may be trusted to hold the scepter for me, a little longer, as his rule is bound to be just and righteous." Thus reasoning, he went away again with his wife and children. They traveled from place to place, not knowing where to go, until, overcome with hunger and thirst, they came at last to a jungle. Here they lived for a time on wild fruits and sweet juicy roots.

Finally, they sought shelter at a wayside inn. Here there happened to be a merchant who had secretly trafficked in human flesh, and, as he gazed with wonder upon the charms of the beautiful Queen, he at once decided to get hold of her and sell her to someone as a bride, so he immediately began to set a trap. He introduced himself to the King and said: "I am a merchant, and have come to do some business a mile from here, and also to secure a house suitable for my wife, who is an invalid and may require a little nursing. Shall we go together to find a little house such as I want?"

The King, who never missed a chance of doing a good turn to a fellow-man in distress, agreed to the plan for the next morning. After some aimless wandering, they found a nice house in a quiet quarter. When everything was settled, they returned to the inn, when the merchant paid his bill, took leave of the King, and pretended to move to his house.

At dusk the merchant sent a sedan chair borne by two men, with a servant and a note to the King, saying: "Dear friend, just as I feared, my wife has arrived ill and terribly upset. May I ask you to be so kind as to send your wife to nurse my wife for the night." The King, who always delighted in good deeds, not suspecting any treachery, allowed the Queen to be taken away to nurse his friend's wife.

The next day, the King, accompanied by the two little Princes, went to the merchant's house, but found no one there. Then the bitter truth dawned upon him. With tears streaming down his cheeks, he searched all over the city for the Queen, but in vain. Then, in agony of despair, leaving her rescue to Divine Providence, he took each of his sons by the hand, and they continued traveling until a stream stopped their progress. The King, unable to get over to the other side with the two Princes, left one on the bank, intending to return and take him across, while he carried the other son on his shoulders while crossing the stream. He had not gone far when a tiger snapped up the son he had left behind and made for the Jungle; then, as the King suddenly turned round to look behind, the boy on his shoulder was jerked into the water and carried away by the current.

Thus, for the King, misfortunes came in battalions. Having lost all his dear ones, he journeyed on by himself, finally wandering into the territory of another Prince, who had just died and his ministers, according to the custom of choosing a successor by lot, took out a hawk and a golden crown and the hawk was let loose just as the woe-stricken King entered the city. After circling round and round over the heads of the crowds, the hawk finally perched on the head of the newcomer. Seeing this, the ministers put the crown on his head and he was installed as King, and so opened a new chapter in his life. He ruled with justice and peace, and plenty smiled upon the land, but the King was sad.

The people knew that the King had no Queen, so to provide him with a companion, his ministers, without consulting him, inquired far and wide for a suitable bride, at the same time promising a handsome reward to the one who found such a person. After a thorough search, one evening a man found a lady in every respect fit to be a Queen, so, after she was approved by the ministers, they left her in a room in the palace, while they told the King about the plan.

It happened that just at this time a hunter and a fisherman brought in two boys, apparently orphans, and as the King, under the Hindu law, is the guardian of all waifs and strays, they were put in charge of his ministers. The boys, left to themselves, except for the presence of the lady, began telling the adventures each had gone through, and while they were talking, the lady in the room leaned forward and listened to their stories, then she suddenly arose and embraced them, and began to kiss them. She was the kidnapped Queen, and the boys were her own two little Princes, miraculously rescued, one from a tiger's jaws and the other from a watery grave.

While the ministers were suggesting matrimony to the King, a messenger came running to the court and informed him of the strange meeting of the lady and her two lost sons. The King, accompanied by the whole court, went to witness the scene, when, lo and behold, whom did he see but his own missing Queen, embracing her two dear sons.

Thus did virtue triumph in the end. The pretended holy man, having ruled the State with harshness, his subjects put him to death. The old ministers found their former Prince and begged him to return to his kingdom, but as he could not be in two places at one time, he cut the Gordian

knot by making each son King of one State with a
council of Elders, the Queen and himself retiring
into private life in accordance with the immemori-
al custom among the ancients.

(Based upon the Story by Shovona Devi.)

Wisdom Gem

REMEMBER THAT VIRTUE always triumphs in the end, even though it may take more than one lifetime. Never become discouraged through suffering and loss. Through your sufferings, learn to sympathize with others and to feel yourself in all. You will enter into your true kingdom at last, in happiness beyond expectation.

— by Paramhansa Yogananda

The Story of a Man Who Was Healed by Suggestion

ne day, a farmer, deep in an interesting conversation with a friend, suddenly looked at the clock and began to foam at the mouth. To the alarmed inquiries of his friend, the farmer said excitedly: "I feel deathly sick. I forgot to bring my opium pills, which I take daily at this hour."

His friend, sensing the seriousness of the situation, quickly assured the farmer that he had some very special opium, which he immediately began in great secrecy to prepare, and soon gave to the grateful man, who, after deeply studying its effect for a few minutes, declared he liked it so much that he wished to use that preparation always. His friend encouraged him to come to his house for the opium from time to time. At the end of a month of interesting experiment, the friend revealed to the farmer that the pills were not opium, but just simple clay and dark water. His slavery to opium was only imagination-born.

Wisdom Gem

MANY SIMILAR INSTANCES can be brought to mind of people who are slaves to imaginary diseases and ailments.

The lesson that this story teaches is that you must cure yourself of evil habits by cauterizing them with the opposite good habits. For instance, if you have a bad habit of telling lies, and by so doing have lost many friends, start the opposite good habit of telling the truth. It takes time to form either a good habit or a bad one. It is difficult for a bad person to be good, and for a good person to be bad, yet, remember that once you become good, it will be natural and easy for you to be good; likewise, if you cultivate an evil habit, you will be compelled to be evil, in spite of your desire, and you will have to pray: "Father, my Spirit is willing, but my flesh is weak." That is why it is worthwhile to cultivate the habit of being good and happy. People seeking happiness must avoid the influence of bad habits which lead to evil actions. Evil actions produce misery sooner or later. Misery corrodes the body, mind, and Soul like a silently-burning acid, and cannot be endured long.

I do not believe that any human being really means to be evil. Why does the greatest criminal do wrong? It is because deep down in his consciousness he does not know better. Even the greatest criminal does not want to hurt himself through his errors. The Sin of all Sins is Ignorance. That is why Jesus said: "Father, forgive them, for they know not what they do." If the criminal, by actual experience of both ways of living could compare his evil way with the right way, would he still continue to follow evil? No. We are all seeking happiness.

Evil cannot keep man under the influence of error forever, because he is made in the image of God. In the beginning, the spiritual aspirant finds his soldiers of discrimination guided by the desire to be good. Later, as he meditates longer and prays ardently for inner help, he finds that the calm conviction of unborn intuition, or awakening Inner Light, a veteran occult General, emerges from the superconscious to guide the forces of discrimination. This awakening Inner Light is the offspring of good Past Habit (Drona).

— by Paramhansa Yogananda

Self-Control

Sadashiva Takes a Vow of Silence

As a young man in his guru's ashram, Sadashiva was a brilliant conversationalist. He often bested in discussion men much older than he. One day, he discomfited an older man by pointing out the inadequacies in his arguments.

His guru demanded somewhat impatiently (or so his words seemed), "When will you learn to hold your tongue?" His disciple's penchant for showing off his intellectual brilliance was a manifestation not only of intelligence, but, less laudably, of ego.

"Instantly, Master, if I have your grace!" came the response. From that day forward, Sadashiva never spoke another word. He became widely known as a mauni of unbroken silence.

Wisdom Gem

IN THE ANNALS of spirituality, there are a few out-
standing examples of obedience. It must be said,
on this point, that a true guru makes every effort
to ensure that his disciple's obedience will be both
deliberate (free-willed) and intelligent, and will not
be a matter of blind or merely submissive acqui-
escence. When this is the case, divine grace flows
freely as it did here, enabling Sadashiva to fulfill
his vow of silence.

— by Paramhansa Yogananda

The Saint Who Ate Fire

Sananda was a great Saint who used to travel across the holy plains of India with a heterogeneous crowd of disciples. Some illumined individuals believe in staying in one place all the time and meditating at the Lotus Feet of the Infinite without undergoing the resultant distraction of continuous travel. Other Saints maintain that it is spiritually necessary to leave each lodging place after a stay of three days at the most, in order to avoid the growth of poisonous inner attachment. The mind is like a blotting paper, which absorbs the color of its contacting environment.

Saint Sananda was of the latter kind and was accustomed to traveling from place to place, depending for his living upon the alms given by the people. In America ministers have to depend upon salaries, or upon free-will financial offerings, while in India, Saints are usually given food, clothing, and shelter. In India, any religious householder considers it a privilege to entertain a real Saint and his disciples.

In ancient times, the Hindu householders used to eat beef or veal, and they used to offer veal, especially to distinguished guests. Later, beef and veal eating was condemned because of the thought that the cow played the part of mother to orphans by supplying them with milk, and because beef and veal eating was found to disturb the Astral and Spiritual vibrations of the human body.

Saint Sananda, with a retinue of forty disciples, arrived at the welcoming home of a rich farmer. According to the then-prevailing custom, a calf was killed especially for entertaining the Saint. The guests in those days were called "Gognah," which signifies "for whom the calves are slain."

Saint Sananda, while he accepted a veal dinner, strictly prohibited his disciples from eating any meat. He explained that they were under training, learning how to control their passions and appetites, and should subsist on fruits, herbs, and vegetables only. He maintained that meat-eating was not good for the morally-uncontrolled and mentally-weak individual, whereas a vegetable diet had a calming effect upon uncontrolled, emotionally-disposed novitiates.

The Saint Sananda ate a hearty veal dinner and took a second helping in the presence of some of his disgruntled, greedy disciples. After the dinner, the Saint ordered the disciples to take up their little bundles, which were fastened on small bamboo sticks and carried over their shoulders, and proceed on a march of fifty miles. After the tedious march started, the Master Saint was always ahead, and kept going round and round to the lagging disciples, urging them to walk cheerfully and with speed, because he wanted to reach the next village before nightfall. Feeling the rebellious vibration of one of the disciples, named Markat who was a combined doubting-Thomas and Judas, the Saint specially exhorted his disciples to let their mental power predominate over the body and dispel fatigue during the hurried march under the rather overzealous tropical sun.

No sooner had Saint Sananda finished his encouraging speech than the wicked disciple, Markat, began to whisper to the other disciples around him: "Look at our teacher and listen to his veal-vitalized speech. No wonder he can walk cheerfully because of his second helping of meat, but think of us. We poor folks are walking with the energy from fruit juices only, and they have already evaporated under the seething glare of the sun."

Saint Sananda, being highly advanced spiritually, was all-knowing, and through his intuition telepathically knew about the doubt-creating, dissatisfaction-generating words of his wicked disciple, Markat. So, he suddenly walked back to Markat, and in front of many other discontented disciples he casually said: "Dear Markat, would you like to eat what *I eat*? Can you digest what I eat?" Disciple Markat, thinking that the Master was going to offer him veal cutlets, emphatically said with assurance: "Honored Sir, just try your food on me and see how fast I can melt it with my digestive fire."

When the forty disciples reached the end of their fifty-mile journey, they were casually told by their Master to tarry a little while around a huge fiery furnace, where a smith was preparing and cutting red-hot nails. On the other side a big calf was being roasted. The Master Saint, being welcomed by the blacksmith, said: "Well, children, sit in a circle around this fire before entering the village, for I am going to offer you some very vitalizing food which I have prevented you from eating for a long time. But before I invite you all to eat, I want Markat to come and sit by me, for he has assured me that he will eat and digest what I eat.

The hungry Markat, beside himself with joy at the sight of the prospective veal roast, leaped to his seat beside the Master Saint. No sooner was the disciple Markat seated than Saint Sananda put his hand into the Pile of red-hot embers and nails and began to swallow them as fast as he could, as if he were eating chopped veal meat. While the Saint was eating these fiery nails and embers calmly, he smilingly but forcefully said to his disciple Markat: "Come on, keep your promise and eat what I eat, and then we will see whether you can digest it or not."

Disciple Markat, highly chagrined and ashamed, hid his face in shame and fell at the feet of his Master, sincerely asking his forgiveness.

Wisdom Gem

THIS STORY ILLUSTRATES that a disciple should follow with faith the discipline enjoined upon him by a true Master. Doubting the motives of a true Master only retards progress in the disciple. Mechanical or willing obedience to the spiritually blind teacher is of little value, for it makes an automaton of an ignorant disciple, but willing obedience to the wisdom-guided will of a Master leads to freedom.

Students, whose wills are governed by their whims, habits, and prenatal instincts, wholly lack the self-control and power to do what is right and consequently cannot obey. Disobedience to the wisdom of a Master, or the voice of Conscience, leads to danger and misery, while obedience to the wise counsel of supermen leads to real freedom and to the attainment of the power to do at will what you think you should do and not what your uncontrolled instincts want you to do.

Do not mechanically follow any stereotyped, unprogressive, incomprehensible, dogmatic teaching, or spiritually stagnant teacher. Make up your mind to find only those Spiritual specialists who, through generations, have scientifically studied all the mystery problems of life and solved them. Learn to find the fountain of all power within yourself and drink of its all-soothing waters, and quench the thirst of your needs.

— by Paramhansa Yogananda

Spiritual Happiness

The Himalayan Musk Deer

usk is a kind of valuable, extremely fragrant salve found in the navel of the musk deer, a habitant of the highest Himalayan Hills of India. At a certain age, the ravishing odor of musk secretly oozes out of the navel of the musk deer. The deer becomes excited at the attractive odor of musk and frisks about, sniffing under trees, and searching everywhere for many weeks to find the source of the fragrance. Finally he grows angry and very restless when he is unable to find the source of the musk perfume, and jumps from the high cliffs into the valley, trying to reach the source of the rare fragrance, and thus plunges to death. It is then that the hunters get hold of him and tear out the pouch of musk.

Wisdom Gem

A DIVINE BARD once sang: "O you foolish musk deer, you sought for the fragrance everywhere but in your own body. That is why you did not find it. If you only had touched your nostrils to your own navel, you would have found the cherished musk and would have saved yourself from suicide on the rocks below."

Don't you think that most people act like the musk deer? As they grow, they seek the ever-fragrant happiness everywhere outside of themselves—in play, temptation, human love, and on the slippery path of wealth, until finally they jump from the cliff of high hope onto the rocks of disillusionment when they cannot find the real happiness which lies hidden within the secret recesses of their own Souls.

If only you would turn your mind inward, in deep daily meditation, you would find the source of all true, lasting happiness existing right within the innermost silence of your own Soul. Don't be like the musk deer and perish seeking false happiness in the wrong place, but, beloved seekers of happiness, awake and try to find your happiness within the cave of deep contemplation.

— by Paramhansa Yogananda

The Philosopher's Stone

A proud prince, with his large retinue blowing trumpets and cow-horns, filed into a jungle of Hindustan, on a pleasure hunting expedition. After bagging many game birds, wild boars, fast-footed deer, and wild, cruel tigers, the prince and his gorgeous party lost their way in the dark womb of the jungle. They had food but no water. They searched and galloped frantically around in the jungle, but they could find no trace of any living water.

As the terrorsome tropical night, with its sinister dangers approached, the Prince and his procession rode madly, seeking shelter. At last, just as the sun was silently fading away, the Prince suddenly came to a crumbling, old cottage. Filled with a faint ray of hope, he pushed the unlatched door open and went in. It was all dark except for a faint glimmer of sunlight which was peeping through a hole in the roof.

Throwing the searchlight of his gaze around, the Prince saw this hole in the cottage roof and he despaired at the horrifying thought that the cottage was deserted. When he was about to turn back and leave the dark cottage, he thought of calling aloud. Hoping against hope to find somebody, he cried "Hello, anybody here?" To his surprise, he heard a calm, firm, peaceful voice reply: "I am here. Do you want water?" The Prince was astounded that this Being could know his thoughts, even before meeting or knowing him.

The Prince and his retinue were beside themselves with joy at being entertained with water and fruits by the holy man of this extremely lonely jungle retreat. The Prince asked the hoary gentleman of the jungle-cottage: "Who are you?" "Well, I am only a poor, old hermit," was the answer. "Aren't you afraid of tigers and snakes?" the prince queried again. "Oh, no, the tigers are my pussycats, and the cobras are my pets. They and I are friends, ever basking in the sunshine of Love, which is in everything."

As the Prince scrutinized the hermit, he was taken aback to see two cobras hanging from his neck in the shape of a garland, but, as the Prince approached to get a closer view of the snakes, they hissed and lifted their hooded heads, ready to express their wrath at the approach of a wrong vibration, for the snakes felt the fear and revengeful spirit hidden in the breast of the Prince.

Just at that time, there was almost a panic among the Prince's followers, as a huge Royal Bengal Tiger came into the cottage and calmly sat down at the feet of the hermit and then slowly slinked away into the dark woods after he received his meed of patting from the hermit.

Amazed still more, the proud Prince thought: "This hoary hermit seems to be good and kind and he saved our lives from wild beasts and parching thirst, so I want to make him rich and prosperous." With this thought in the back of his mind, he materialized his thoughts into articulate words, saying: "Hoary hermit, your face is beaming with kindness and sincerity. I appreciate all that you have done and I am going to tell you a secret of becoming very rich, a secret which I am going to reveal for the first time, only to you." With this, the prince pulled out a Philosopher's Stone from beneath his folding garment and again addressed the hermit: "I am going to entrust you with this family Philosopher's Stone for a year so that you may become rich by using it. This gold-making stone was given to my father by a great mystic alchemist and it has the power to convert into gold anything you touch with it. Use this every day to convert all the stones and rocks into gold for a whole year and build a golden palace here. Then I will come back again to pay you a visit and get my precious Philosopher's Stone, which I value more than my life. And for Heaven's sake, don't lose it."

The hermit did not want to accept the responsibility, but somehow consented to keep the stone at the Prince's repeated vehement importunities. The Prince saw the hermit casually tuck the Philosopher's Stone under the light band of clothing at his waist. (Many people in India carry their money that way — safe from the reach of pickpockets.)

The Prince went away, and after a year had passed he came back again with his retinue, to the self-same cottage of the hermit, but expecting to see a palace. He was stricken with horror as he saw the same cottage but in a greater state of decay. He got down from his charger, rushed through the open cottage door, and shouted: "Hey, hermit, are you alive?" A deep, sonorous voice responded "O, yes, Prince. Welcome to my humble home."

Without any ceremony of delay, the Prince shouted: "What is the matter with you? What did you do with my Philosopher's Stone? Why didn't you use it to become rich?" The hermit scratched his head and replied: "Well, well, what do you mean about my remembering a stone? I don't want to be richer." The Prince, beside himself with rage and terror, demanded: "Don't you remember the gold Philosopher's Stone which you tucked beneath your waistband a year ago? What have you done with it?"

"Oh yes, now I remember all about that precious stone of yours. I happened to be immersed in the deep thought of Spirit and went to bathe in the river, and it must have dropped out then."

Upon hearing this, the Prince, crying: "I have lost everything," fell into a swoon. The hermit brought him back to consciousness by sprinkling cold water on his face. The Prince's retinue demanded the death of the "careless thief of a hermit," as they called him. The hermit laughed and said: "You hydra-headed man, I didn't know that you would make such a fuss about a stone. Come along with me to the river and let me search for it."

The Prince derisively replied: "Well, search for the stone after it slipped in the swift currents of the river a year ago?" The hermit, undaunted, commanded with a loud voice: "Princeling, and all of you, come on. Don't make another fuss until we have searched the riverbed."

Under the spell of a strange magnetism, the Prince and his retinue, in utter muteness, followed the hermit to the river. Then the hermit asked the Prince to pull out his handkerchief and hold its four corners with his hands and dip it into the waters of the river and cry out: "O Prince of the Universe, Maker of all precious stones, give me back my Philosopher's Stone." As the Prince raised his handkerchief out of the water, he beheld two score of Philosopher's Stones, exactly like the one he had lost. With unbelieving, amazed eyes, he came out of the water and found by testing each stone that each one could convert other stones on the shore into gold.

Then the Prince tied all the two score gold-making stones in his handkerchief and threw them back into the river. The hermit and the retinue cried out: "Hey, hey, why did you do that?" The Prince turned to the Saint, fell at his feet with folded hands and said: "Honored Saint, I want to have what you have, having which, you regard gold-making stones as worthless pebbles."

So the Prince left his Kingdom in order to acquire the imperishable Kingdom of Spirit.

Wisdom Gem

THIS STORY ILLUSTRATES that earthly riches, no matter how valuable they may seem, are perishable and have to be left behind after the body grows cold. Instead of wasting your time only in using your Philosopher's Stone of gold-making business ability, to acquire perishable riches, you should be like the hermit, who had the imperishable riches of God. Having God, you will be wealthy beyond dreams, and, if necessary, will throw away millions of earthly money like pebbles in order to acquire the imperishable riches of Spirit.

— by Paramhansa Yogananda

Non-Attachment

A Fearful Disease

n a village in India three people died un-accountably of some disease. The villagers, distressed, repaired in a group to a solitary *sadhu* (holy man) who lived outside the village, and asked him to intercede. The sadhu meditated, and found that the disease had been caused by a demon. He summoned the demon and told him, "This village is under my protection. Leave it alone." The demon promised to obey.

A week later, at least a hundred other people had died. It seemed a veritable epidemic. Again the villagers approached the sadhu and cried, "Your prayers have not helped us. There must be a terrible curse on our village!"

The sadhu summoned the demon again and scolded him, saying, "I told you this village is under my protection. You promised to leave it alone. Now it appears you have broken your promise."

"No, I haven't, Holy One!" protested the demon. "It's true I killed the first three, but all the others died out of fear."

Wisdom Gem

EVENTS THAT AFFECT others need not affect oneself,
or at least not in the same way: The secret, in this
case, is to maintain an attitude of non-attachment,
not reacting emotionally. Indeed, emotional reac-
tions can greatly augment any karmic effects.

The ultimate way to escape the results of all
karma is to "evaporate" the causative ego, with its
consciousness of identification with the little "cup"
of the body. In deep meditation, that vapor of ego
may rise and disappear altogether in the sky of
infinite consciousness.

If the dragon strikes, and you are no longer
there for it to seize you in its jaws; or if the rock
falls from on high but you have removed yourself
from the spot where it falls; or if the fickle multitudes acclaim you (and, inevitably, expose you
later on to the dualistic opposite of public oppro-
brium) and you are not there to respond: What
happens? The same actions occur, but they will
not occur to you.

— by Paramhansa Yogananda

The Man Who Wounldn't Be King

ong ago, there lived a few Saints in a retreat at the outskirts of a jungle valley. Here they ate the fresh fruits from trees, and drank, with the cup of their hands, the living water of the sparkling mountain springs. Here blew the zephyr of ceaseless peace, and their diamond-eyes glittered with celestial smiles. Joy throbbed in their bosoms, giving perpetual solace.

And yet, one day, one of the Saints thought he had had too much of spiritual happiness and wanted a little taste of kingly happiness. He wanted to be a king for a day. With this desire scorching his heart, he set out in quest of regal happiness, and left the satisfying, peaceful nook of the hermitage.

On the way he thought: "Heavenly Father, I am Thy child, surely Thou wilt guide me to the place where I can enjoy kingly happiness for a day." Thinking this as he walked some distance from the hermitage, his eye fell upon a stately, palatial mansion. "Ah, I see the Heavenly Father has made my dream come true," he exclaimed, and began hurrying toward the mansion.

He passed by the gates and wasn't stopped by any of the guards; he walked all over the flower-bedecked garden, and he met no one. He went into the dining room of the palace and found steaming hot, delicious food invitingly awaiting him at the table, but not a trace of waiters or servants. Encouraged by all this strange array of edible food, he thought: "The Lord is good to me and has materialized this palace and wonderful food fit for a king just for me. It is just as I wanted. My dreams have come true."

Being sentimentally convinced, he proceeded to enjoy the preliminaries of being a God-sent king for a day.

He took his bath in the royal bathroom, dressed, then sat down for dinner. At this time the servants of the palace, who had been out gambling, rushed in and in great excitement shouted: "Who are you, eating the food of our king who is out hunting and is expected to arrive any minute?" The Saint, still thinking that it was a test of the Lord, and thinking himself to be a cosmopolitan friend, replied in a calm, loving tone: "I am a friend of the Great King; I have come here at His command to enjoy royal happiness for a day."

The servants, taking the Saint to be an august

guest of their king, let him finish the royal dinner and ushered him to sleep in the royal chamber. They did not understand that the Saint referred to God as the "Great King" and not to their earthly king who was out hunting.

Two hours passed. The herald of the king arrived with a message from His Highness, stating that he was detained and would arrive at the end of three hours and would like to have steaming hot food prepared. The servants anxiously asked: "Didn't his highness send a guest to enjoy his dinner and bed?" The king's herald was frothing at the mouth with rage when he found that this beggar-Saint without invitation had devoured the king's food and was audaciously snoring on the royal bed. So, he urged the servants to run out and bring sticks, staves, and broomsticks with which to rout the beggar-Saint.

The Saint was awakened from his dream of royal happiness by sticks and staves mercilessly falling upon him, but the more the servants beat him and scolded him, the more he laughed without cessation. The servants became furious at his increasing laughter and flogged him to unconsciousness and threw him beyond the palace gates.

The unconscious Saint was picked up by a brother Saint and was taken back to the hermitage. The brother forced milk into the mouth of the unconscious Saint, and by way of testing his recovery of consciousness, asked: "Do you know

who is feeding you milk?" The beaten Saint laughingly replied: "The same God who beat me for
trying to be a king for a day — that same God is
feeding me milk."

The brother hermits were glad to see their
chastised brother Saint's faith in God unchanged in
prosperity (as when he found repose in the king's
bed) and in adversity (as during his subsequent
punishment). This beaten Saint wasn't like those
who worship God during prosperity and disbelieve
in God during adversity.

Meanwhile, the king of the palace returned to
his mansion and demanded hot food, and was
very wrathful to learn of the beggar who had eat-
en his food and who had laughed when he was
being beaten. The whimsical king took a fancy to
the strangeness of the story of this audacious beggar, and ordered his servants to find him. The servants searched high and low until returning home
in despair, they galloped past the Saint's retreat
and were attracted by his loud laughter. They dis-
mounted, kidnapped the beggar Saint, and took
him before the king.

When the king and the Saint met, the Saint began to laugh louder than ever, as if unable to hold
his merriment within the cup of his heart. The king
repeatedly asked the Saint, under threat of death,
the reason for his laughter while being beaten.
When threats failed, the king used entreaty, and,
being driven mad by curiosity, offered his throne

to the beggar if only he would explain his laughter while being beaten.

At last, seeing the king humbled, the beaten beggar Saint replied: "Look, I was thrashed by God for craving the delusive enjoyment of kingly material comfort for a day, but my laughter increased because I 'got off easy.' I thought: If I merit so much beating for just one day of being king, think how many more beatings are coming to that king for indulging in kingly material happiness for years! I was beaten for forgetting God for just one day, but think how much beating you yet must have, in one form or another, for forgetting Him every day — all the time! No, thank you, I would not be king, for I have ever-fresh happiness in God, which does not end with the lashing of worries."

Wisdom Gem

THE SOURCE OF lasting happiness is living for God and with God no matter what life places before one.

If, along the journey through life, you are aware that you are being led by desire for personal fulfillment, even so, proceed with God in your heart. Pray for Him to be with you and guide you. In this way desires will naturally lose their power of attraction when compared to the divine sweetness. Always express a joyful and heartfelt gratitude to the Divine Giver of all.

— by Paramhansa Yogananda

The Wishing Tree

nce upon a time there was a hermit of Hindustan named Hari, who wore the soles off his feet traveling through the rocky regions of the Himalaya Mountains in search of a certain wishing tree. The Indian legends describe this wishing tree as grown by fairies and endowed with great and trusting qualities, and specially endowed with magic powers. Such miracle-making trees are said to have been grown by divine fairies for the benefit of true hermits who might happen to seek them.

Hermit Hari was spiritual, devoted, and firm in his determinations. Long had he searched for God but had received only glimpses of Him in meditation. Next to God, the coveted object which Hermit Hari searched for was the wishing tree, which was supposed to grant the fulfillment of any or all desires to the one who sat under it.

It seemed that, although Hari had failed to commune with God at will, nevertheless he had grown great occult powers due to his austerity, self-discipline, and occasional contacts with God. It seemed that the time had at last arrived when Hermit Hari's determined search had culminated into the accumulation of good *Karma* (action.) Through the magnetic power of the stored-up good Karma and latent divine power manifest in Hari, he felt that he was going to be rewarded through the possession of a wishing tree.

Hermit Hari's bud of a wish seemed to grow into a flower of fulfillment when he apparently accidentally came across a great bushy tree in the course of his travels in the interior snow-walled valleys of the Himalayas, where very few people were able to desecrate this virgin magic land with their sordid footsteps. His strange intuition at once led him to recognize at first sight that this large bushy tree was a wishing tree. Suddenly, inspired by untold delight he raced toward the tree, and standing under it as per the magic directions, he wanted to test the occult powers of this famous "wishing tree."

Hermit Hari said to himself: "If it is a wishing tree, I desire the instantaneous materialization of a mighty castle." No sooner had he expressed the wish than the great castle suddenly materialized beside the tree, spreading out over a vast area as if it had always been there.

Encouraged by the first success of his test with the wishing tree, he made another wish: "I would like to be attended by bright-eyed damsels and fairies serving me food on golden plates." This also came to pass. Encouraged still further by the instantaneous fulfillment of so many of his long-unfulfilled desires, Hermit Hari then wished for a mighty army to protect him and lo, there appeared a mighty army guarding the great castle.

After dinner, Hermit Hari retired to a secluded room on the ground floor of the castle. This room was rather dark and dreary, and as Hermit Hari lay there looking toward the open window which overlooked the forest, he sent forth another strong thought: "I am protected by an army of soldiers but the window in my room is open without bars. If a tiger comes and gets me, that will be the finish."

Just then, as Hermit Hari continued in his attitude of fear, a big tiger bolted through the open window of the castle bedroom and carried off the fear-frozen Hermit Hari. It was too late for him to realize that he was under the influence of a wishing tree which would grant both his good and his bad wishes, irrespective of whether they were actuated by good or undesirable motives. The business of a wishing tree is to grant wishes, and it was true to form, according to the strength of thought, whether negative or constructive.

My great Master often used the above story to illustrate that we all are living in this world beneath our magic-all-desire-fulfilling wishing tree of will power. Our will, being a reflection of the Almighty Divine Will, has in it the seeds of almightiness.

Wisdom Gem

MOST PEOPLE REJOICE if, as the result of a continuous will and effort in an unknown past life, they suddenly succeed in this life, but most people, by continuously misusing their will power, suddenly reap evil consequences and forget that they were created by their own wishing tree of almighty will power. It is wise to wish for good things while you are standing beneath the almighty wishing tree of your will, and be careful that you do not concentrate upon fears, failures, diseases, ignorance and lack of God-contact. They might suddenly loom out of the unseen and cause you unending troubles.

Remember, you were born beneath the boughs of the wishing tree of high accomplishments and achievements and you must not think evil, as that will bring nothing but harm to you. Since you are under the Invisible Wishing Tree of the Divine Will in you, use it all the time to learn of God and attain Self-Realization. In this way you will forever quench the thirst of all your desires.

— by Paramhansa Yogananda

The Woman Who Loved God as Her Son

*M**any are the astounding stories** told about Krishna, the Christ of India. He lived several centuries before the Christian Era. Around His life, clusters many stories parallel to the life of Jesus. Krishna's parents were prosecuted by King Kansa, and King Herod caused trouble for the parents of Jesus. The Christ and Christna or Krishna stories have a great deal of similarity. Jadava, the Christna, and Jesus, the Christ, have great Spiritual concomitance.

Jadava, the Christna, signifies Jadava, the man, who could project his consciousness into all the Cosmos. Jesus, the Christ, signifies also that Jesus had expanded his consciousness into Cosmic Consciousness. Jesus was born of devout parents, so, also Krishna was born of God-fearing parents. Jesus conquered Satan; Krishna conquered the demon Kaleo (Ignorance), which was destroying people by its venom. Jesus stopped the storm; Krishna lifted a hill over a village like an umbrella and prevented it from being flooded to destruction.

Jesus was called "King of the Jews"; Krishna was a real king of the high caste Brahmins and a large earthly kingdom. Jesus and Krishna both were unmarried. Jesus had his women devotees, Mary and Martha; Krishna had Radha and the Gopis. Krishna taught one of the greatest philosophies of India in the Bhagavad Gita; Jesus taught one of the greatest Western philosophies in the Christian Bible. Jesus was crucified by being nailed to the cross; Krishna was shot to death by an arrow. Jesus and Krishna both performed miracles and both are recognized as the greatest incarnations of God. The word "Christ" was used in India in connection with those who had attained Cosmic Consciousness long before Jesus was born and designated as the "Christ." So, Jesus, being an Oriental born after the time of Christna, also got the same epithet.

There are many ways in which a devotee can worship God. In the Western World, the Father and Son relationship between God and the worshiper is prevalent. In India, the Mother and Son relationship between God and the devotee is preferred because the father's love is conditioned by reason, whereas mother's love is not conditioned by anything. The greatest sinner is still a son, to his mother.

When God is invoked as a Divine Mother, the devotee removes all the diffidence born of the consciousness of sin and thinks: "Well, Divine Mother, naughty or good, I am Thy child, and as such must find forgiveness under all circumstances, no matter what I have done."

There are other unusual relationships in which God can be known, and these are described in the Hindu Scriptures. God can be worshiped as a lover, as a beloved, as a friend, as a Divine servant, as a Master, or as a son.

It is said that the great woman devotee, Jasoda, wanted to look upon God as her Son, so she in time came to adopt Christna, the great incarnation of God. Baby Krishna was full of childish pranks, yet He was the "apple of the eye" of the milkmaids and the people who lived with Him in the sacred village of Brindaban. One of Krishna's favorite pastimes was to push the milkmaids, who carried the milk in large goblets on top of their heads, so that the milk pots slanted and poured milk like young Niagara Falls into the open mouth of the waiting Krishna below. The milkmaids never complained, but loved to be taken by surprise by Krishna, so that he might have the milk.

Young Krishna used to be very fond of cheese, so one day he secretly took an unusually large piece of cheese and began to run. After a long chase through the winding corridors of the house, Mother Jasoda caught hold of Him, but it was too late, because Krishna, afraid to lose his cheese, put the whole big piece in his mouth, so that his cheeks

puffed up the size of a small football. Krishna tight-
ly closed his lips, but the relentless Mother Jasoda,
afraid that her Divine Immortal Son, Krishna,
would be choked to death, forcibly pried his jaws
open with her fingers in order to pull the cheese
out. Baby Krishna laughed and opened his mouth,
but behold, there was no cheese there. To her
amazement, Mother Jasoda saw, not the cheese but
a Tunnel of Eternity, with the stars and worlds moving there amidst fire, smoke, and thunder!

Mother Jasoda immediately shouted: "Nay,
nay, Lord Baby Krishna, close your mouth and
have your cheese. I don't want to know you as
God, but only as my godly baby. Christna closed
his mouth and apparently swallowed the cheese
and, saluting his mother, went away to play with
his neighborhood playmates.

Wisdom Gem

ONCE AN IDOL of salt tried to measure the ocean by diving into it. It found itself melting away and losing itself, so it came out of the ocean to tell its friends its experience with the ocean. "Dear friends," it said, "I don't want to lose myself in the ocean, and yet I wanted to know the ocean without losing myself. Now I know that the ocean is briny and very deep, and before I melted I pulled myself away." This illustrates the characteristics of some devotees who dive into the ocean of Spirit just to discover its depth, but who pull out before they lose their individual identity in God.

Mother Jasoda, as she looked into the Tunnel of Eternity, the spaceless forest of vastness blazing with unending light, found herself melting into it, so she pulled away from it and preferred to see God materialized in the definite, tangible form of Krishna. God is Finite and Infinite both. God and Creation emphasize the finiteness of God. God with Creation dissolved into Him, reflects Infinitude. Some devotees like the finite expression of God, whereas others prefer the Infinite aspect of the Divine. Mother Jasoda loved and found God in her Son, Krishna. God fulfills all the desires of devotees, as the earthly mother satisfies all the wholesome desires of her children.

— by Paramhansa Yogananda

The Power of Delusion

he following story was often shared by Swami Kriyananda. He heard it from his Guru, Paramhansa Yogananda and expresses here his guru's important commentary.

There is a saint, Baba Haridas, who lived in the eighteenth century. He was buried underground with his nose sealed for forty days to give testimony to the state of breathlessness. Numerous precautions were put in place to insure the validity of the experiment. When they brought him up after forty days he was lifeless and presumed dead. Some French physicians examined him and said, "Yes, he's dead now." Then, suddenly, exercising the will power of his soul, Haridas wakened. Baba Haridas had realized certain *siddhis* (powers) that had allowed him to perform this feat.

One time a Christian missionary was in a boat with him and Baba Haridas asked this Christian missionary, "What can your Jesus Christ do that I can't do?" Well, because they were in a boat, the missionary said, "He could walk on water." And Haridas said, "Is that all?" And he got out of the boat and walked on the water and the boat followed him wherever he went! Indeed, he certainly had acquired some miraculous powers. But you know, an interesting thing was that the maharaja of that particular country was not fooled. He said to some friends of his, "I know you all think very highly of this man, but I feel there's something wrong." He could feel that there was still ego there.

One day Baba Haridas ran away with a woman and lived with her for a while. After some time, he realized he'd made a mistake and came back to his disciples. He said, "I'm sorry that I left you and now I've come back." Even so, Baba Haridas found liberation in that life, so my Guru said. I know a disciple of my Guru who asked the question, "But isn't the punishment much greater when you fall from a high state?" And my Guru said, "God is no tyrant. He doesn't judge the way we do." God saw that this person really didn't want anything, he didn't want that stale cheese, he wanted fresh and good cheese, he wanted God. It wasn't a question of forgiving him. He just took him back. But, this Baba Haridas did have that ego and did fall. You have to be afraid of that possibility because there's always the danger that you will fall into delusion. You have to watch yourself. You're not safe until the very end. When you've reached Nirbikalpa Samadhi, then you are free.

Wisdom Gem

THE MORE YOU want, the less you have. You don't have riches if you're looking for them. Be complete in yourself. A wonderful way to affirm this in your own life is the following. Every night, before you go to sleep, sit in meditation. When you've achieved a certain level of calmness in your meditation, mentally build a fire and cast into that fire every seed of desire. Remember all the things that you wanted and no longer desiring them, offer the heartfelt words, "No, I don't need that." Consider all that you're attached to and with truthfulness say, "No, I don't need that." "This is not I." You will gradually come to see, and it's a very natural thing, that you become freer and freer and more aware of your oneness with God.

— by Paramhansa Yogananda

The Man, the Donkey, and the Boy

man, his donkey, and his boy were going to the market to sell the donkey. Because the donkey was going to be sold, they didn't ride it so that it would be fresh and perky and sell for a better price. They met a group of people walking the other way, and one of them said, "Look at that, a perfectly good donkey to ride, and they're walking! What fools!" And the man thought well, I don't want to be an object of ridicule, so he got on the donkey. Another group came by, "Ah, look at that! Here that healthy man is riding while his poor little child is struggling along beside him." So the man said, "Well, there is something in that, so he put the little boy on the donkey and he walked alongside. And another group came by, and said, "Look at that ridiculous situation, that young boy with young legs who could easily walk, and the poor old man is hobbling along beside the donkey."

So the man thought, well, okay, I don't want to be an object of scorn, and so he got on the horse too, and both of them were now riding as they started to cross a bridge on their way to the marketplace. Another group came by, and you know just what they would say, even if you don't know the story! "Look at the cruelty to that poor animal! Two people on that one little donkey." And the man was so fed up with it, he just pushed the donkey off the bridge and walked home!

Wisdom Gem

DON'T WORRY ABOUT what other people think and do, about their common sense objections. Mind you, it's so easy to object if one doesn't have to do something themselves. They don't have to live with the decision or the result, so they're willing to give any advice they like.

Try to be more centered in yourself. Try to feel in your heart what is right for you. Don't worry about others.

— by Paramhansa Yogananda

The Farmer Who Dreamed His Sons Were Killed by a Cobra

There **was a farmer standing** by a tree, absorbed in thought. His wife came rushing up, weeping, to announce that their only son had just been killed by a cobra. The farmer made no reply. Stunned by his seeming indifference, the wife cried, "You are heartless!"

"You don't understand," the farmer replied. "Last night I dreamed that I was a king, and that I had seven sons. They went out into the forest and all were bitten by cobras and died. Now I am wondering whether I ought to weep for my seven dead sons in that dream, or for our one son who has just been killed in this dream we are dreaming now."

Wisdom Gem

THE FARMER WAS a man of spiritual vision. To him, the material world and the subconscious dream-world were both equally unreal.

When we dream at night, this present dream fades into unreality, and only that subconscious dream-world seems real to us. When we return again to the dream of this world, that other dream is forgotten.

Everything exists only in consciousness.

— by Paramhansa Yogananda

Truthfulness

Guru (Preceptor) Nanaka

*T*he great *Divine Reformer, Saint* Nanaka, was dropped on earth like the soothing dew of Heaven to quench mankind's thirst for knowledge. Irrespective of caste and creed, the Hindus and Mohammedans flocked around his banner. Though Hindus and Mohammedans have diametrically opposite religious customs and beliefs, yet they were soulfully treated alike by this great Saint Nanaka. No Spiritual Victrola or over-talkative reformer had ever been able to mollify the crude differences of belief of the alliterative fanatics of Hindu and Mohammedan religions.

Nanaka lived the life of Truth, and by extreme piety and virtue personified it in his actions. He gave both the Hindus and Mohammedans a chance to behold in manifestation the comforting universalities underlying the two religions. Nanaka, by his miraculous power and exemplary conduct, dissolved the bigoted beliefs of his heterogeneous followers and established in their hearts the Oneness and Omnipresence of God and the spirit of universal Brotherhood.

One day, Nanaka, during the service hour in the Mohammedan Mosque, instead of bowing down in front of the altar, lay down with his feet toward the altar and his head away from it, and feigned that he was asleep. The fanatic Mohammedans, who indulged in demonstrative external modes of worship, instead of concentrating upon God, beheld through the corners of their squinted eyes the audacity of this strange man, Nanaka, who lay down instead of sitting, who slept instead of praying, and above all, who was sacrilegious enough to put his feet, instead of his head, toward the altar.

The leader of the Orthodox coterie, almost beside himself with wrath, came to Nanaka and upbraided him for putting his feet toward the altar: "You audacious sinner, take your feet away from the altar of God. If you don't, your feet will rot."

Calmly, collected, with the Infinite power trembling in his voice, authoritatively Nanaka demanded "Pray tell me, which way shall I put my feet — where there is no altar of God's Presence? I behold Him north, south, east, west, above, beneath, within, and without, and all around me. If you could only show me a place where God is not there, I would be only too glad to shift my feet to that place. Your outwardly praying minds do not feel God even on the altar in front of you. Your minds are roaming over the hills of restlessness. Correct your indifference to God. Your heads are toward the altar, but your Souls and minds are away from God. I am glad that even my feet are in the all-protecting, all-guiding power of God."

The priest, apparently vanquished, unable to reply to the Master's admonitions, became almost beside himself with wrath again, and said: "Sinner, you must take your feet away from the altar of God." He took hold of the feet of Guru Nanaka and forcibly turned them away from the altar, but behold, a miracle occurred. With the turning of the feet from the west to the east, the altar and the whole temple wall moved toward the north.

When this happened, the priest's followers demanded their leader to be humble and to recognize the great power of this God-known man. Thus the leader and his religious band lay prostrate at the feet of the Master Nanaka. Then Nanaka blessed them and said: "Ye children of my Omnipresent Father, realize the presence of God within yourself first, in the best altar of your heart, and if you find him there, through that inner window, you will find God nesting in Omnipresence. To localize God at one point is to imprison Him within the walls of finitude. Those who confine God in the walls of their imagination never find Him. Those who break the walls of sense-experience with the hammers of all-dissolving, intuitive silence, find God spread out in uncaged space everywhere.

Wisdom Gem

JUST AS THE confined water rushes in all directions
when the walls holding it are broken, so also when
the embankments of bigotry and restlessness are
broken, the consciousness of man spreads out and
expands into the Omnipresent consciousness of
Spirit.

— by Paramhansa Yogananda

The Saint Who Went to Hades Speaking Truth

seraphic Saint, who lived in a forest, was wont to sit in the shade of a huge tree, immersed in deep contemplation. At the call of dawn, the Saint would rouse his sleeping spirit and offer it to God. One morning, when the dew drops were sobbing their dying farewell to the tender blades of grass; and the Saint was musing on the joy of his just-finished meditation, his attention was slightly distracted by the sound of footsteps fast approaching him.

The Saint was so calm that he did not even care to look around to ascertain the cause of the noise. However, in a few moments a man with an acute fear-distorted face halted for a moment in front of him, and in an imploring voice said: "Honored Saint, supreme lover of Truth and truthful actions, please do not tell my pursuing bandit enemies my hiding place in the tree above you or they will kill me." Saying this, the much-frightened man almost ran up to the top of the tree and hid there within its kind sheltering leaves.

The Saint remained silent, saying neither yea nor nay to the entreaty of the frightened man, so the man naturally thought that silence meant consent and that the virtuous man would not betray him, which betrayal might result in his death.

However, as the man lay hidden atop the tree, the Saint began to struggle within himself as to what he should say, according to the advice of the Scriptures, which he followed very strictly and literally. He thought: "The Scriptures say not to speak an untruth, so I could not say, if questioned by the enemies of the pursued man, that I do not know where he is. No, I would rather cut off my tongue than indulge in lies."

Then he thought of the entreaty of the pursued man and the consequence resulting in murder if he spoke the truth. Puzzled as to how to choose between speaking an untruth and the murderous result of speaking the truth, the Saint at last determined within himself: "If the bandits question me about seeing their prey, I shall say: "I know where he is but I will not tell you. Do what you like." Thinking this, the Saint sat all prepared to meet the difficult predicament.

At last the vicious bandit leader, with his retinue, arrived, and finding that the Saint was the only man within range of his vision, he gruffly said: "Hey, angel, I will not molest you if you will tell us whether you know the hiding place of the man we seek."

The Saint thought that by remaining silent the bandit would stop questioning him, but that plan did not work, for the bandit-leader meant business and began to beat him. When severe beatings did no good, the bandit-leader flashed out his sword from its scabbard and brandished it before the Saint and gave him five minutes to make up his mind After that, the bandit swore that the saintly body would sit forever still under the tree, but without a head.

A severe mental struggle ensued in the mind of the Saint as to what he should do, and at the end of the five minutes the Saint replied: "I know where your man is hiding but I won't tell you."

"Well," the bandit jeeringly replied, "beating and flashing of the sword has made you break your silence and now, behold you will tell the truth to me." Saying this, the bandit cut off one of the Saint's hands and said tauntingly: "I will give you five minutes more in which to tell the truth, or your head will dance on the earth in a pool of blood."

Then the Saint began to hunt for scriptural injunctions as to what he should do and he remembered one scriptural passage: "Protect your own self above all things, for that is most important. You must live first above all, in order to achieve your highest ambition of finding God. If you die for not telling the truth (when you should tell the truth) you are a fool." So, at the end of the five minutes, when the bandit leader was about to chop off his head, the Saint raised his finger upward and showed the bandit the hiding place of the sought-for, doomed man.

Forthwith one of the bandits clambered up the tree, dragged the unfortunate man down, and hacked him to pieces limb by limb in front of the Saint. While this man was being murdered, he shouted at the Saint: "Mr. Saint, you will see Hades for this." However, the Saint thought that he had done his duty in saving his own more serviceable, greater Soul as compared to the less useful, less developed Soul of the pursued man, and thus he rejected the curse of the dying man as foolish and absolutely unlikely to ever happen to him, who had followed nothing but the Truth.

At last, years later, when the Saint consciously left his body in the ecstasy of Cosmic Consciousness, his Astral body arrived in the Kingdom of Heaven. Immediately, Jama, the keeper of Hell, visited him in Heaven and told him that before he could get the final sovereign orders of the Supreme Spirit to live in Heaven, he must witness the loathsome Hades. Disturbed, the Saint replied: "Honored Jama, this is outrageous. I have lived a moral life with mathematical accuracy, weighing each action from the standpoint of Truth. I have always followed Truth and performed truthful and just actions, I know

I don't deserve the punishment of visiting Hades even for a short time."

The great Jama replied: "Honored Sir, no doubt you are right about yourself in everything except one act. You say you never did anything but what was truthful and just. Why is it that you were foolish enough to get your arm cut off and the head of a man cut off for stating a fact? I am afraid that you are all mixed up about the difference between Justice and Truth and the pronouncement of a fact. A just and truthful action always results in good, whereas your statement of a fact, which resulted in great harm to yourself and to that man, was far from ultimate Truth and Justice.

Why didn't you point your finger in the wrong direction in the forest and save yourself from harm and also save the life of a man? Do you realize that even if you had committed the sin of uttering a falsehood, that would have been less sinful than the horrible sin of being an instrument, help, and supreme factor in the murder of an innocent man who sought and believed in your shelter? By your silence, you let the hiding man think that you would protect him and then, in order to save yourself, you betrayed him and deprived him of the opportunity of seeking another hiding place unknown to you."

Jama continued: "Honored Saint, know this, from now on, that a truthful action always results in true, good results, and is different from the statement of a fact which may produce good or evil. Always give preference to an action which results in good, as compared to a statement of a fact which may result in severe harm. To call to a lame man or a blind man: "Hey, Mr. Lame Man," or, "Hey, Mr. Blind Man," may be the statement of a fact but would be unwholesome, unjust, and untruthful in effecting what is good, whereas, to say: "Hello, Perfect One," or "Hello Strong Man," or "Hello, Man of Spiritual Vision" in calling the lame, or halt, or blind, may not be a statement of fact, but such statements are truthful and wholesome in effect. Therefore, they are the Truth.

Follow Truth in preference to the statement of crude facts which result in harm to yourself or others, but, remember at the same time, that it is not good to indulge in cheap lies. Suppose you were a Saint and you were meditating in your room and I secretly and quietly saw you doing so and I came to your door and knocked, and when you opened the door I inquired of you: "Mr. Saint, what were you doing," and you replied: "I was eating bananas," then I would know that you were a cheap liar, who tried to hide from me the fact that you were meditating.

In the above case, you sacrificed my trust by trying to be modest through the means of lying. If you had answered my question with: "Well, I was just a little busy," you would not have spoken an untruth, but you would have evaded the Truth.

The result of this would be that even if I happened to discover and knew that you didn't tell me the Truth, I couldn't accuse you of lying. I couldn't even blame you for evasion.

Honored Saint, one should avoid cheap prevarication, and may distort facts only in those cases where it is a question of life and death, and a person unjustly accused of murder can be saved from the gallows. To dilly-dally or equivocate in telling an untruth, which might save a life, amounts to stating a fact which might involve the loss of that life and is evil and should be avoided.

Develop the habit of speaking the truth without unnecessarily advertising all your secrets, for, if you tell about your own weaknesses to unscrupulous false friends, they will have great times poking fun at you whenever the occasion arises, even though they may possess to a greater degree the same weaknesses which you possess. Speak Truth; speak pleasant Truth, avoiding the unwholesome, fact-stating habit which may result in serious trouble for yourself and others.

Speak and act in a way that will bring lasting happiness to yourself and others. Avoid cheap lying and the habit of prevarication, for by this habit you will lose the trust of everyone. It is permissible to speak an untruth or hide facts if a good person's life can be saved thereby, or a person unjustly accused of murder can be saved. You should know the difference between Truth which ultimately brings good to all concerned, and the statement of facts which may result in atrocious troubles for yourself and others.

Avoid repeating unpleasant Truths; for instance, calling a sensitive man a human idiot. Do not tell all the facts of your life. You may relate the truthful ways of life which you have followed, which will bring forth good to yourself and to all people."

Wisdom Gem

REMEMBER HOW THE Saint went to Hades for stating an unpleasant, unwholesome, evil-producing fact, which resulted in extreme evil, and for not knowing the difference between a good-producing statement of Truth and the evil-producing statement of a fact. The idea is that, even if a man does not believe in Hades, he must know that this earth and one's own misguided mind can be made hotter than any Hades and that this earth and one's own mind can be sweeter than Heaven by following the path of righteousness. If you speak an unpleasant Truth, or state some unwholesome fact that may result in the murder of a man or of his Soul, then your conscience will trouble you as long as you live for not saving the man's life behind the thick screen of prevarication.

— by Paramhansa Yogananda

Devotion

The Story of Sri Chaitanya

soteric activity means to do everything
with the consciousness of God. Work with your
heart calm and full of love. "My feet are purified
walking for Thee; my voice is sanctified talking
of Thee; my feelings are pure, feeling Thee. Work
Thou through my hands and my feet, through my
eyes, my brain, and my speech."

Calmness is the throne of God. Meditate day
and night and do not lose that power. As often as
you think, bring back that power. My Master said:
"There are willing instruments and unwilling instruments. God works through willing instruments."
So do not obstruct His power.

When you drink God, endless throngs of intox-
ication are with you. That silent, burning devotion
comes to you. Pray silently until He answers you.
Pray when others are asleep: "Father, answer my
heart-burning prayers. I am no longer satisfied
with playthings, Father, I want Thee. I will wake all

Creation with my cries. Come, I want Thee. Play-things no more!"

Devotion is the love expressed to God. Devotion must not have fear. It is to your own interest that you should show devotion to God silently, devotion of the heart, burning devotion. Surrender yourself to Him and pray until He answers you. No one can destroy the charm of Divine Love.

Now the great Saint, Sri Chaitanya, shall use my speech, my voice, my thoughts, my brain, everything to express his devotion as follows:

"Way, way long ago, I, Chaitanya, came to India, I didn't preach any sermons. I didn't talk of anything but the love of God. The burning love of God expressed wherever I went, I talked no wisdom. I only spoke as I felt, but thousands followed me just to hear me say two or three words, as follows: 'Radha, Radha, Radha Govinda jaya Radha' 'Spirit and Nature, Spirit and Nature dancing together. Victory to Spirit and Victory to Nature.'

"Nature is the consort of my Beloved Father, and my Father is the Spirit. Those two phases I saw everywhere, and I wanted to speak of their love in all — the love of the mother and the child, the love of the father and the mother, the love of man and woman, and the love of all things.

"As I was walking through the village, I was singing, 'Victory to Spirit and Victory to Nature.' And as I was singing this in the streets, men and women left the village and followed me, but as I was going along I lost sight of them and came into a vast field, where a washerman was washing some clothing and I said: 'Washerman, washerman.' He said: 'Don't talk to me, I am too busy; get away, you mad man.' But I said: 'You have got to talk to me. All I ask you to do is to sing. Give me the happiness of singing my Beloved's name and then I will go.'

"So, I sang and he sang with me: 'Victory to Spirit and Victory to Nature,' and the washerman sang, and all the clothes he was washing fell from his hands and he followed me, singing, and the birds sang of their love of Nature and God. And as we went singing, the wife of the washerman came and said: 'What is the matter, you follow that crazy man?' And the washerman said: 'You may beat me up, but sing just once with me.' And the washerwoman sang, and we all sang, and the broomstick dropped from the washerwoman's up-lifted hands. And we all sang: 'Spirit and Nature, Spirit and Nature.'

"Then four village gossips came along and they cried: 'Hey, what is the matter? You follow that crazy man and your husband?' The washerwoman said: 'That is all right. You sing once with me.' And we all sang: 'Spirit and Nature, Spirit and Nature,' and those broomsticks dropped from their hands. One hundred, two hundred, three hundred, five hundred, all came to drive us away as we sang while going through the village, but I walked off with all of them."

Wisdom Gem

"So, DEAR ONES, don't take the name of God in vain. Sing, live, and drink the name of my Beloved and get all drunk with His name. Let us all sing, as I sang long ago, of the love of God. Hearts aflame, souls afire. 'Radha, Radha.' Sing on! Sing on! 'Spirit and Nature, Spirit and Nature — I will sing Thy name, I will drink Thy name, and get all drunk with Thy name.'"

May the bliss of Lord Chaitanya be with you — every one. Sing His name with all your heart. No more with a dry voice and absent-minded prayers; drink His name, and get all drunk with His name!

— by Paramhansa Yogananda

Radha, the Greatest of the Gopis

adha was the greatest of the gopis. Krishna felt free, therefore, to demonstrate his selfless, divine love for her, though in reality he gave that love equally to all.

There came a time when the other gopis grew jealous of Radha. Krishna decided to teach them a lesson.

One day Radha happened to be absent, but the other gopis were all clustered about him. Suddenly with a groan he cried, "Oh! Oh! I have a terrible headache! Please, won't someone do something for me?"

"What, Lord?" they cried in desperation. "What can we do? We'll do anything!"

"If only one of you will press her feet on my head, my headache will go away."

The gopis gasped in horror. In India, to place one's feet on the head of someone senior to one-self is considered insulting. To place them on the

head of the guru is sacrilegious. In deep conster-
nation the gopis looked away. None dared to offer
her services.

And all the while, Krishna's headache kept
growing worse.

After some time had passed, Radha appeared.
She learned of Krishna's distress. "What can I do
to help, Lord?" she cried anxiously, as the others
had done.

"Please, just press your feet on my head!"
Krishna cried. "Nothing else will help me."

"But of course, Lord. Instantly!" replied Radha.

"No! No! You mustn't!" cried the other gopis.

"Why on earth not?" inquired Radha.

"If you do," they warned her, "you will go to
hell!"

"Is that all that's worrying you?" Radha scoffed.
"Why, if pressing my feet on our Lord's head will
give him one moment of relief, I will gladly go to
hell for eternity!"

She was about to do as he had asked, when
Krishna sat up smiling. His headache was gone.

And then the other gopis understood. They
had been concentrating on their own safety, not
on Krishna's well-being. Now they all bowed before Radha's greater, because selfless, love.

Wisdom Gem

THOSE WHO LOVE others selflessly are already on the way to learning the secret of divine devotion. All they need is to direct that love upward, to God.

— by Paramhansa Yogananda

Willpower

The Holy Squirrel

*I**t does not seem possible** that we, who are made in the immortal image of God, can cease to exist at death. Neither can we think that imperfect beings can, at death, all at once merge into the being of God. It stands to reason that if we are cut off by untimely death in an imperfect state, we shall have to be reborn on earth in order to wash away all our stains of error before we can merge in God as His Perfect Image.

Of course, men seldom reincarnate as animals. That would be devolution instead of evolution. In rare instances it happens that a person who has lived a very brutish, animalistic existence is drawn into the body of an animal to learn some lesson. This explains the "thinking dogs" and "thinking horses" which have puzzled scientists who have tested them.

But this story is based on an entirely different principle. It is said that a great saint or teacher who is highly evolved can *deliberately* assume the form of an animal in one or more incarnations. To prove that God is omnipresent, some saints have worked not only through human vehicles but also through the vehicles of lower animals even as electricity can work in the human body as well as in a mechanical machine. God operates the life of humans, animals and atoms; saints who become one with Him demonstrate that they also can operate through human bodies, animal bodies, and atoms. This was demonstrated by Jesus when he put his omnipresent life into the dead body of Lazarus. He also demonstrated that he could shut off the Life Force by making the fig tree barren. He thus proved that he had the power to put on or shut off Life Force at will. Jesus, having atomic control, also fed many people with a few loaves of bread. Saint Francis also had power over animals in that the birds obeyed him and listened to his sermons and flew away in the form of a cross while a vicious wolf became friendly and ceased its carnivorous habit through the divine influence of St. Francis, who by his omnipresent consciousness, awakened the sleeping God in the wolf and changed its nature.

Therefore, just as a saint can influence animal bodies, so he can encase himself, or reincarnate, in any sort of body. The Scriptures and literature of India contain many stories of such incarnations. So, I hope you will understand the theme of this

story about the reincarnation of one of India's holy
Saints in the body of a mother squirrel.

This Saint, who had lived as a recluse, so loved
baby squirrels that he wanted to incarnate as a
mother squirrel so that he could actually bestow
his maternal affection on the helpless little ones.
The story tells how this Saint reincarnated as a
holy mother squirrel and with her tiny babies lived
on the top of a tree by the sea. Devotees soon realized that this was not an ordinary squirrel, but that
the furry little body housed a great Soul who had
reincarnated thus to demonstrate the will of God
even in the animal body. So, many people learned
of this unusual mother squirrel, and it is said that
whosoever fed her either became prosperous, or
was healed of whatever affliction he possessed.

Once upon a time, when the holy squirrel had
gone far away from the shore in quest of food, a
storm lashed the ocean into high waves and swept
away the tree with all the baby squirrels. The loving mother, on her return, discovered the dark
work of the sea and commanded: "Ocean, give me
back my babies or I will destroy you."

When the ocean paid no attention to her warn-
ings, the mother squirrel was seen, day and night
for seven days, dipping her bushy tail in the water
and then brushing it on the sand.

Seeing this continuous, curious, determined
activity, an Angel of God appeared and said: "Holy
mother squirrel, of all the strange things, your

action of dipping your tail in the ocean and rubbing it on the sand is the strangest. Please tell me the reason for your queer activity."

The squirrel replied: "Heavenly Angel, the audacious sea swallowed my babies in my absence and paid no heed to my request to return them, so I am resolved to run the ocean dry." The Angel laughed and remonstrated, "Why, mother squirrel, in seven days more you won't have any brush left on your tail with which to attempt to run the ocean dry!"

But the tiny mother, with the determination of Eternity written on her face, replied: "A thousand million lives or more will I be born again and again as a squirrel, and I will grow as many bushy tails as are required to dry the ocean." Saying this, the holy squirrel went on with her strange activity.

Seven days later, the brush of her tail had almost disappeared, and yet the mother squirrel had not stopped her work. In fact, the dynamic will — in tune with Divine Will perfected in former incarnations, had prepared her to continue as long as the world endured. And so the Angel of God came back, and with folded hands said: "Holy squirrel, your will is law; please stop punishing the ocean and we will return your babies."

Only then did the mother squirrel rest.

Wisdom Gem

REMEMBER, DEAR STUDENT, if all mortal methods of seeking happiness have failed you, do not be discouraged, but rouse your slumbering, all-accomplishing divine determination. Then you will find that the Divine laws of God are bound to give you the dream-happiness that you desire.

— by Paramhansa Yogananda

The Bandit and the Bull

nce upon a time a very evil bandit named
Rakusha lived with his gang in a cave hidden away
in the dark breast of the hills of northern India.
This rapacious robber was noted for his cruelty and lived by pillage, murder, and plunder. He
was by nature very vicious. It is said that the tiger
will go on killing animals even though it may be
gorged to the throat with meat — just for the fun
of killing. This tiger bandit excelled in the art of
cruelty and shunned and ridiculed every spiritual
law that he happened to think of. He was the incarnation of wickedness. A sample of his supreme
perversity can, in a small measure, be seen from
the following event.

Once this master-bandit started with his band
on a mission to plunder a poor little village at the
outskirts of a forest. As he passed through the forest, he carried on an orgy of killing the songbirds
just for the thrill of it. When he arrived at the end of

the forest, he perceived a dirt road half a mile long leading into the village. This road was shaded with an avenue of tall trees. One of the bandit gang remarked that the avenue of tall trees afforded shade to the travelers from the heat of the sultry Oriental sun. "Well," the bandit-leader remarked: "all of you get busy and circle those trees, cutting their bark, and letting them die, so that they may no longer be liberal with their shade to the villagers."

His orders were obeyed, and as the band of robbers were about to enter the village they found that they had to walk over loose bricks laid in a muddy puddle of water. After they had crossed this puddle, the bandit-king thought: "Let me remove the bricks lest anyone else utilizes the comfort of walking over them and thus misses an unpleasant contact with the mud. However, on second thought, he refrained from doing this, as he suddenly remembered that he had to walk over the bricks again himself on his way back to his den beyond the forest.

In the meantime, as this bandit and his followers were entering the village, a few Saints happened to be going out of the village and they were delighted to walk on the bricks in the mud puddle, thus saving their sandals from getting soiled. Now, fix in your minds this incident of the holy men crossing the mud puddle, using the bricks unwillingly left there by the bandit-king for his own selfish purposes.

The bandits plundered the village, slaughtering the men, women, and children, and once again started on their return. Once again the bandit-king had to walk on the bricks over the mud puddle. After he and his gang were through using the bricks, the leader, with his long spear, pushed them into the deepest holes of the mud puddle, lest anyone else should try to use them.

Now the scene changes. Shortly after this, the bandit-leader was treacherously killed by one of his subordinates, who wanted to be at the head of the robbers' roost. It is said in the Hindu Scriptures that every man has two Angels (with two recording books) invisibly residing at his left and at his right shoulders. The Angel on the left side writes in his book all the misdeeds of the man, and the Angel on the right side records all his virtuous actions. So, when the Soul of this most atrocious robber was being escorted to the darkest and most hideous part of Hades, the leader in charge of Heaven and Hades, to make sure that no injustice was done, asked the two Angels to look into their records. The Angel on the left side said: "Honored Sir, the book of sin is so full of this man's wicked deeds that I had to write all around the margin of all the pages of my book."

The Angel on the right said: "All the pages of my book are blank. I cannot find a single record of good action performed by this cruel bandit." Being asked to re-examine his book thoroughly, the Angel on the right exclaimed: "Ah, I find on the last page a single, indirect, virtuous action. This bandit once unwillingly left a few bricks in a puddle of mud so that he might re-cross over them, and he has a reward coming to him because a few holy men happened to use those bricks to cross the puddle."

Then the Angel in charge of Heaven and Hades said to the bandit Soul: "You have two hours of complete freedom in Heaven or Hades. Pray let me know your last wish." The bandit Soul, still gorged with wickedness, thought it over and harshly growled: "Get me a flying bull from Hades with long, sharp-pointed horns." The ferocious flying bull arrived. The bandit got on the bull's back and, being assured that the bull would do just as he commanded, he said: "Mr. Bull, charge all the keepers of Hades." There was wild havoc. Hades had never had such an uproar and confusion.

Hearing of this confusion, the Angel in charge of Heaven and Hades, with his flying assistants, arrived on the scene to save the attacked keepers of Hades. The bandit Soul, in great glee, stopped pursuing the Hell-keepers and at once ordered the bull to drive his long horns into the body of the Angel Leader. Seeing this inevitable doom approaching him, the Angel and his assistants began to fly all over space, racing to find shelter behind Heaven's safe gates. The keepers in Hades sent telepathic broadcasts to Heaven, telling the Angels about this terrible outrage caused by the super-bandit.

Archangels flocked to the rescue of the fleeing Angels, but, according to the decree, none could withstand the attack of this flying bull, who was working havoc under the supreme command of this very wicked bandit Soul. The scene was extremely embarrassing and ludicrous, to see even the most powerful host of Angels, including the keeper of Heaven and Hades with his assistants, fleeing for their lives toward Heaven.

The bull entered the Pearly Gates hot on the heels of the fleeing Angels. Heaven was in an uproar. At last, just as the fleeing Angels and the bandit on the flying bull reached the Golden Throne of His Majesty, the two hours had passed, and suddenly the bull stopped his outrageous activity of goring the Angels at the command of the bandit Soul. The Angels folded their wings and rested. But the keeper of Heaven and Hades approached the powerless bandit and shouted: "So, even in this other world you had to follow your wicked way. We will give you and your flying bull overtime work in the worst part of Hades. Heaven is too good for you."

Suddenly, the Angels and all were frozen into stillness as the Heavenly Father exclaimed: "No, you will not throw the wicked bandit and his bull back into Hades, because they are already free, for they have reached Heaven. It doesn't matter how anyone gets here, even if it is by only a very little goodness, he shall never go to Hades again."

Wisdom Gem

AND SO, DEAR friend, by its audacity, this strange story is designed to help you remember no matter what you have been in the past, if you sin no more and cultivate even a little goodness, that may be the portal to the Heaven of eternal joy and freedom. The idea is, do not keep brooding over the distance between you and Truth, but keep walking toward it by doing some good every day, and you will finally reach your goal.

— by Paramhansa Yogananda

Wisdom

Getting Out of Delusion

A **certain man in ancient India** was being harassed by a demon. He decided to use a Vedic mantra to banish this pest. Taking a handful of powder, he uttered the mantra over it, infusing (as he thought) the powder with mantric power. He then cast the powder on the demon. The demon only laughed. "Before you could even recite your mantra," it mocked, "I got into the powder myself. How, then, could your mantra harm me?"

Wisdom Gem

So YOU SEE, the very mind with which you would banish delusion is already steeped in the very delusion you want to overcome! It is not always easy, even, to know right from wrong. Introspection helps, and is, indeed, essential. Even more important, however, is the intuitive guidance of a wise guru, especially from within.

— by Paramhansa Yogananda

Six Blind Men and the Elephant

hat tractors are to this country, elephants are to India. In impassable places, checkered with unending paddy fields, moats, and irrigation canals, these elephants serve as huge, black, village tractors. The elephant is a free-booter, hence it can walk through canals, culverts, and ditches just as you and I can wade through little puddles and holes after a severe rain. The elephant carries huge logs and breaks trees in twain with his mighty trunk; in other words, serves the purpose of a mighty tractor.

The elephant, caparisoned with right furnishings and a *howdah* on its back, offers a comfortable, gorgeous throne for the luxury-loving princes of India. Princely coronations and magnificent processions are meaningless without elephants. Tame elephants are employed to catch wild ones. And the elephant ivory tusks make wonderful articles with which to pamper the love of luxury of the rich. On the other hand, the elephant eats up whole forests of leaves and consumes vast quantities of rice and other food, so that only a prince can afford to maintain these mammals.

The elephant is a true friend and an unforgiving enemy. In the Orient it symbolizes wisdom, due to its intelligence. Also, elephants are made to perform wonderful tricks such as standing on their hind legs, picking needles up with their trunks and so forth. It is said, of one of the Hindu Gods, that he had the head of an elephant and the body of a man, like a Centaur, half man and half beast. This elephant-god, Ganesh, represents the God of success through worldly wisdom.

There are numerous legends and stories about elephants. Even the philosophers of India used the elephant to illustrate a great moral, as the following story will show:

In India, the elephant is usually driven by a driver called a "Mahout." The mahout elephant-driver puts his feet on the two large fan-like ears of the elephant and directs the course to the left or right, or ahead, or to halt, by the different kinds of pressure of his feet on the elephant's ears. When the elephant is stubborn and lazy in his travels, he is made to hurry by the prick of an iron hook held in the hands of the mahout.

Once upon a time an elephant-driver commanded his six blind sons to wash the family elephant. The six blind boys took great pride in this opportunity offered them by their good father, and each boy was extremely careful in the diagnosis of his first experience with the elephant while washing him. Each boy was given a certain portion of the elephant's body to wash, and each boy was beside himself with joy, thinking that he knew what the elephant looked like.

After an hour, when the elephant-wash was over, each of the blind sons simultaneously shouted: "I know all about the elephant." The first son said to the second son: "Well, what is the elephant like?" The second brother, who had been washing the sides of the elephant, shouted: "Oh, the elephant is just like a huge wall." The first son, who had been washing the elephant's trunk, scornfully said: "You are talking nonsense. The elephant is just like a bamboo pole."

The third son, who had washed the elephant's ears, listening to the quarrel between his two brothers, laughed and shouted: "Hey, you fools, you don't know anything. The elephant is like two big banana leaves."

The fourth son, who had been washing the four legs of the elephant, hearing what he thought to be absurd remarks from his brothers, cried out: "You are all wrong. It is ridiculous for you to fight about something you know nothing about. The elephant is nothing but a huge roof of flesh supported by four fleshly pillars."

The fifth son, who had been washing the tusks of the elephant, and was beside himself with laughter, cried out: "You blundering fools, listen to me. I declare with absolute experience that the elephant is nothing but a couple of bones."

The sixth son, who had washed the tail of the elephant, burst into hysterical laughter, crying out: "You all must be crazy or under the spell of hallucination. The elephant is only a piece of string hanging from Heaven." The sixth son, being the youngest and quite short, could not reach to the top of the elephant's tail, hence he thought that the elephant was a "Heavenly string," very much alive, being suspended to earth by the gods.

The father, who had been cooking some rice for the elephant in a nearby place, heard in great merriment all this squabble about the elephant and came running to his children when their argument had waxed into a free-for-all fight. He shouted at the top of his voice, crying: "You assorted young fools, stop this fighting and *know that you are all right and that you are all wrong.*

The six sons in unison cried: "How can that be?" To which the father replied: "It is I who have seen the whole elephant, and I know that you are all right because you have each one described a part of the elephant, but you are all wrong because the whole elephant is neither a couple of tusks, or four legs, or one trunk, or a huge wall of flesh, or a tail, but he is an aggregate of all of these. The tail, or the trunk, separated from the elephant, could not be termed an 'elephant'."

Wisdom Gem

THIS STORY VERY well illustrates the condition of modern theoretical religions and "isms." Most religious denominations are more or less blind, possessing only partial knowledge of the whole elephant of Truth. That is why, most of the time, bigoted religionists, like the six blind men, keep flying at one another's throats, claiming to know the whole Truth. Each denomination thinks that its teaching is the only teaching, and holds in ridicule all other teachings existing beyond its boundary.

The time has come when people can heal their inner blindness by awakening the latent Christ-wisdom within them through meditation, the feeling of brotherhood, understanding, and the light of their own inner Self-Realization. When the blindness of ignorance and denominational prejudice is healed by the Self-Realization of God, then the whole elephant of Truth will be perceived as consisting of the essence of all religions. Then inter-denominational wars and religious and racial prejudice will cease, and there will be one church, one brotherhood, one scientific highway of religions, and one Temple of Truth everywhere.

— by Paramhansa Yogananda

That Moral Backbone

ong ago there lived a poisonous hooded snake near a rock outside a village. This reptile killed many of the children in the village with its death-dealing fangs, and every attempt of the villagers to kill this sly snake failed. So, as a last resort, the villagers visited their holy man, who lived in a secluded spot in the village, and demanded: "Holy Master, please use your spiritual powers to prevent the snake from continuing its gruesome work of murdering our little children." Thereupon, the Saint agreed to comply with their request.

Finally, the holy man went near the place where the snake lived, and by the magnetic power of His Divine Love induced the snake to come out. Then the Saint commanded: "Mr. Snake, desist from biting to death my dear people of the village. Practice non-violence." With humbled hood the snake promised.

The Saint then went on a pilgrimage. After a year, as he was returning to the village, he passed by the rock where the snake lived and he thought of the snake, wondering if it had kept its promise. To his astonishment he found the snake lying in a pool of blood with severe wounds in its back.

When asked what was the matter with him, the snake in a feeble voice replied: "Holy Preceptor, I have seven wounds in my back as a result of your teachings. Ever since the village children found out that I was harmless, they have pelted me with stones whenever I went out in search of food. I ducked in and out of my hole many times but still I received seven injuries in my spine. Master, at first they fled at sight of me, but now, due to your teachings of non-violence, I have to flee from them."

The Hindu Master patted the snake on the back and healed him, and then smilingly rebuked him, saying: "You little fool, I told you not to bite, but why didn't you hiss?"

Wisdom Gem

So, REMEMBER, WHEN you are too much imposed upon by people and friends who want to get the best of you, do not be spineless, and yet do not inject the poison of injury into them, but, rather, keep them at a distance by the use of a few firm statements.

— by Paramhansa Yogananda

The End

Index:
Stories Listed by
Their Spiritual Qualities

Index:
Spiritual Qualities Listed
by Their Stories

Bibliography

Kriyananda, Swami. "God Alone," Retirement Speech, Portland, Oregon, May 5, 1996.

Kriyananda, Swami. *The Hindu Way of Awakening.* California: Crystal Clarity Publishers, 1998.

Kriyananda, Swami. "The Man, the Donkey, and the Boy," Sunday Service Talk, Palo Alto, March 5, 2000.

Kriyananda, Swami. "The Power of Delusion," The Bhagavad Gita Talk (#61) 2010.

Yogananda, Paramhansa. "The Bandit and the Bull," *Praecepta Lessons*, 1934, Vol. 1: #9.

Yogananda, Paramhansa. *The Essence of Self-Realization.* California: Crystal Clarity Publishers, 2009.

Yogananda, Paramhansa. *The Essence of the Bhagavad Gita.* California: Crystal Clarity Publishers, 2008.

Yogananda, Paramhansa. "The Fisherman and the Hindu Priest," *Praecepta Lessons*, 1938, Vol. 3: #56.

Yogananda, Paramhansa. "Guru (Preceptor) Nanaka," *Praecepta Lessons*, 1935, Vol. 2: #29.

Yogananda, Paramhansa. "The Himalayan Musk Deer," *Praecepta Lessons*, 1934, Vol. 1: #12.

Yogananda, Paramhansa. "The Holy Squirrel," *Praecepta Lessons*, 1934, Vol. 1: #13.

Yogananda, Paramhansa. "The Man Who Wouldn't Be King," *Praecepta Lessons*, 1934, Vol. 1: #11.

Yogananda, Paramhansa. "The Most Humble God," *Clarity Magazine*, (Spring 2013): *Praecepta Lessons*, 1934.

Yogananda, Paramhansa. "The Philosopher's Stone," *Praecepta Lessons*, 1935, Vol. 2: #40, #41.

Yogananda, Paramhansa. "The Reward of Virtue," *Praecepta Lessons*, 1938, Vol. 4: #100.

Yogananda, Paramhansa. "The Saint Who Ate Fire," *Praecepta Lessons*, 1938, Vol. 3: #53.

Yogananda, Paramhansa. "The Saint Who Went to Hades Speaking Truth," *Praecepta Lessons*, 1935, Vol. 2: #30.

Yogananda, Paramhansa. "Six Blind Men and the Elephant," *Praecepta Lessons*, 1938, Vol. 3: #72.

Yogananda, Paramhansa. "The Story of a Man Who was Healed by Suggestion," *Praecepta Lessons*, 1938, Vol. 3: #67.

Yogananda, Paramhansa. "The Story of Sri Chaitanya," *Praecepta Lessons*, 1938, Vol. 4: #96.

Yogananda, Paramhansa. "That Moral Backbone," *Praecepta Lessons*, 1934, Vol. 1: #7.

Yogananda, Paramhansa. "The Three Gods and the Lord of Gods," *Praecepta Lessons*, 1935, Vol. 2: #39.

Yogananda, Paramhansa. "The Wishing Tree," *Praecepta Lessons*, 1938, Vol. 6: #135.

Yogananda, Paramhansa. "The Woman Who Loved God as Her Son," *Praecepta Lessons*, 1934, Vol. 1: #22.

About the Storyteller — Author Paramhansa Yogananda

"As a bright light shining in the midst of darkness, so was Yogananda's presence in this world. Such a great soul comes on earth only rarely, when there is a real need among men."

—His Holiness the Shankaracharya of Kanchipuram

Born in 1893, Yogananda was the first yoga master of India to take up permanent residence in the West.

Yogananda arrived in America in 1920 and traveled throughout the country on what he called his "spiritual campaigns." Hundreds of thousands filled the largest halls in major cities to see the yoga master from India. Yogananda continued to lecture and write up to his passing in 1952.

Yogananda's initial impact on Western culture was truly impressive. But his lasting spiritual legacy has been even greater. His *Autobiography of a*

Yogi, first published in 1946, helped launch a spiritual revolution in the West. Translated into more than a dozen languages, it remains a best-selling spiritual classic to this day.

Before embarking on his mission, Yogananda received this admonition from his teacher, Swami Sri Yukteswar: "The West is high in material attainments but lacking in spiritual understanding. It is God's will that you play a role in teaching mankind the value of balancing the material with an inner, spiritual life."

In addition to the *Autobiography of a Yogi*, his spiritual legacy includes music, poetry, and extensive commentaries on the Bhagavad Gita, the Rubaiyat of Omar Khayyam, and the Christian Bible, showing the principles of Self-realization as the unifying truth underlying all true religions.

Widely considered one of the 20th century's most influential spiritual teachers, his life and work helped launch and inspire a spiritual revolution. By the turn of the century, thousands of seekers around the world considered themselves his disciples.

Further Explorations

Crystal Clarity Publishers

If you enjoyed this title, Crystal Clarity Publishers invites you to deepen your spiritual life through many additional resources based on the teachings of Paramhansa Yogananda. We offer books, e-books, and audiobooks, a wide variety of inspirational and relaxation music composed by Swami Kriyananda, and yoga and meditation videos.

See a listing of books below or visit our secure website for a complete online catalog, or to place an order for our products.

Crystalclarity.com
800.424.1055 | clarity@crystalclarity.com
1123 Goodrich Blvd. | Commerce, CA 90022

Ananda Worldwide

Crystal Clarity Publishers is the publishing house of Ananda, a worldwide spiritual movement founded by Swami Kriyananda, a direct disciple of Paramhansa Yogananda. Ananda offers resources and support for your spiritual journey through meditation instruction, webinars, online virtual community, email, and chat.

Ananda has more than 150 centers and meditation groups in over forty-five countries, offering group-guided meditations, classes and teacher training in meditation and yoga, and many other resources.

In addition, Ananda has developed eight residential communities in the US, Europe, and India. Spiritual communities are places where people live together in a spirit of cooperation and friendship, dedicated to a common goal. Spirituality is practiced in all areas of daily life: at school, at work, or in the home. Many Ananda communities offer internships where one can stay and experience spiritual community firsthand.

For more information about Ananda communities or meditation groups near you, please visit **Ananda.org** or call 530.478.7560

The Expanding Light Retreat

The Expanding Light is the largest retreat center in the world to share exclusively the teachings of Paramhansa Yogananda. Situated in the Ananda Village community near Nevada City, California, it offers the opportunity to experience spiritual life in a contemporary ashram setting. The varied, year-round schedule of classes and programs on yoga, meditation, and spiritual practice includes Karma Yoga, personal retreat, spiritual travel, and online learning. Large groups are welcome.

The Ananda School of Yoga & Meditation offers certified yoga, yoga therapist, spiritual counselor, and meditation teacher trainings.

The teaching staff has years of experience practicing Kriya Yoga meditation and all aspects of Paramhansa Yogananda's teachings. You may come for a relaxed personal renewal, participating in ongoing activities as much or as little as you wish. The serene mountain setting, supportive staff, and delicious vegetarian meals provide an ideal environment for a truly meaningful stay, be it a brief respite or an extended spiritual vacation.

For more information, please visit **Expandinglight.org** or call 800.346.5350

Ananda Meditation Retreat

Set amidst seventy-two acres of beautiful meditation gardens and wild forest in Northern California's Sierra foothills, the Ananda Meditation Retreat is an ideal setting for a rejuvenating, inner experience.

The Meditation Retreat has been a place of deep meditation and sincere devotion for over fifty years. Long before that, the Native American Maidu tribe held this to be sacred land. The beauty and presence of the Divine are tangibly felt by all who come here.

Studies show that being in nature and using techniques such as forest bathing can significantly reduce stress and blood pressure while strengthening your immune system, concentration, and level of happiness. The Meditation Retreat is the perfect place for quiet immersion in nature.

Plan a personal retreat, enjoy one of the guided retreats, or choose from a variety of programs led by the caring and joyful staff.

For more information or to place your reservation, please visit **Meditationretreat.org**, call 530.478.7557, or email **Meditationretreat@ananda.org**

The Original Writings of
Paramhansa Yogananda

1946 Unedited Edition
of a Spiritual Masterpiece

AUTOBIOGRAPHY OF A YOGI
Paramhansa Yogananda

Autobiography of a Yogi is one of the world's most acclaimed spiritual classics, with millions of copies sold. Named one of the Best 100 Spiritual Books of the twentieth century, this book helped launch and continues to inspire a spiritual awakening throughout the Western world.

Yogananda was the first yoga master of India whose mission brought him to live and teach in the West. His firsthand account of his life experiences in India includes childhood revelations, stories of his visits to saints and masters, and long-secret teachings of yoga and self-realization that he first made available to the Western reader.

This reprint of the original 1946 edition is free from textual changes made after Yogananda's passing in 1952. This updated edition includes bonus materials: the last chapter that Yogananda wrote in 1951, also without posthumous changes, the eulogy Yogananda wrote for Gandhi, and a new foreword and afterword by Swami Kriyananda, one of Yogananda's close, direct disciples.

Also available in Spanish and Hindi from Crystal Clarity Publishers

SCIENTIFIC HEALING AFFIRMATIONS
Paramhansa Yogananda

Yogananda's 1924 classic, reprinted here, is a pioneering work in the field of self-healing and self-transformation. He explains that words are crystallized thoughts and have life-changing power when spoken with conviction, concentration, willpower, and feeling. Yogananda offers far more than mere suggestions for achieving positive attitudes. He shows how to impregnate words with spiritual force to shift habitual thought patterns of the mind and create a new personal reality.

Added to this text are over fifty of Yogananda's well-loved "Short Affirmations," taken from issues of *East-West* and *Inner Culture* magazines from 1932 to 1942. This little book will be a treasured companion on the road to realizing your highest, divine potential.

METAPHYSICAL MEDITATIONS
Paramhansa Yogananda

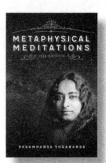

Metaphysical Meditations is a classic collection of meditation techniques, visualizations, affirmations, and prayers from the great yoga master, Paramhansa Yogananda. The meditations given are of three types: those spoken to the individual consciousness, prayers or demands addressed to God, and affirmations that bring us closer to the Divine.

Select a passage that meets your specific need and speak each word slowly and purposefully until you become absorbed in its inner meaning. At the bedside, by the meditation seat, or while traveling — one can choose no better companion than *Metaphysical Meditations*.

∼ WISDOM STORIES series ∼

Yogananda knew that stories have a way of opening our hearts and minds, making connections the intellect alone may miss. He told these tales to illustrate the spiritual and practical truths he was teaching. Not only to be inspired but also able to apply those teachings to our daily lives. Each individual story in this series, is followed by a "Wisdom Gem," illuminating spiritually vital qualities such as Right Action, Courage, Unconditional Love, Faith, and Wisdom, in an enjoyable way to explore and reflect on these universal principles.

STORIES FROM INDIA, VOLUME ONE
Paramhansa Yogananda

In volume 1, Paramhansa Yogananda's treasury of Indian tales will delight both the casual reader and students of Eastern thought. Featuring a gamut of characters-from saints to thieves, God-realized masters co lions and frogs-these stories were all told by the Master himself in his lectures, informal talks, and writings.

Whether you are a teacher, parent, student, or devotee, these stories are an excellent resource to turn to again and again for inspiration, sharing, and personal study.

∼ MOMENTS OF TRUTH series ∼
Little Books, Big Wisdom!

This series — excerpts from some of the greatest scriptures of our time — takes spiritual truths and makes them easily accessible. The small, pocket-sized editions let you bring these nuggets of wisdom with you on your travels — whether on pilgrimage or to the workplace. Start and end your day with one of these inspirational gems from *The Rubaiyat of Omar Khayyam Explained*, *Autobiography of a Yogi*, *The Essence of the Bhagavad Gita*, and more!

Selected Offerings

THANK YOU, MASTER
Hare Krishna Ghosh, Meera Ghosh, and Peggy Deitz

Anyone who has read and loved *Autobiography of a Yogi* will be delighted to find this treasure of personal experiences and heartfelt remembrances of Paramhansa Yogananda by three of his direct disciples.

Stories from Yogananda's family members, Hare Krishna Ghosh and Meera Ghosh, who became disciples as teenagers, take the reader on pilgrimage to India to the sacred places and miraculous moments shared with this great yogi. The stories of Peggy Deitz transport one to Yogananda's ashram in California and his time living with devotees in America.

Whether humorous or miraculous, casual or divine, these accounts bring to life the experience of being in Yogananda's presence. They give insight into the profound love with which he guided each individual.

Firsthand experiences from close disciples are a true gift that can help us tune into his vast nature. At the same time, these delightful stories will touch your heart and uplift your spirit.

SHAPED BY SAINTS
Devi Mukherjee

While a young man, Devi Mukherjee worked with Mahatma Gandhi in the Indian resistance movement and was imprisoned for five months. After his release, Devi began a spiritual quest throughout India, traveling some forty-five years at various times.

From 1955–66, he was part of the Yogoda Satsanga Society, Yogananda's organization in India. There, he and Swami Kriyananda were brother monks. He later married the daughter of Yogananda's childhood friend Tulsi Bose. The Mukherjee family lived in Tulsi's former house in Calcutta, where he and Yogananda dreamed and meditated as boys.

Devi takes the reader on a profoundly inspiring pilgrimage to meet saints and realized masters of modern India in forest ashrams, mountain caves, holy places, and shrines. He shares many insights and lessons from the great ones and tells many previously unpublished stories of Yogananda's early life and return visit to India in 1935–36.

PARAMHANSA YOGANANDA
A Biography with Personal Reflections and Reminiscences
Swami Kriyananda

Paramhansa Yogananda's life was filled with astonishing accomplishments. And yet in his classic autobiography, he wrote more about the saints he'd met than about his own spiritual attainments. Yogananda's direct disciple, Swami Kriyananda, relates the untold story of this great master and world teacher: his teenage miracles, his challenges in coming to America, his national lecture campaigns, his struggles to fulfill his world-changing mission amid incomprehension and painful betrayals, and his ultimate triumphant achievement. Kriyananda's subtle grasp of his guru's inner nature reveals Yogananda's many-sided greatness. Includes many never-before-published anecdotes and an insider's view of the Master's last years.

THE ESSENCE OF SELF-REALIZATION
The Wisdom of Paramhansa Yogananda
Recorded, compiled, and edited by his disciple, Swami Kriyananda

Filled with lessons, stories, and jewels of wisdom that Paramhansa Yogananda shared only with his closest disciples, this volume is an invaluable guide to the spiritual life carefully organized into twenty main topics.

Great teachers work through their students, and Yogananda was no exception. Swami Kriyananda comments, "After I'd been with him a year and a half, he began urging me to write down the things he was saying during informal conversations." Many of the three hundred sayings presented here are available nowhere else. For anyone wishing to know more about Yogananda's teachings and absorb his wisdom, this book and *Conversations with Yogananda* are must-reads.

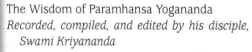

Be assured that at each sitting, whether for one page or one chapter, you will have gleaned some refreshment for a tired heart or a thirsty soul. . . . *Essence* is easy to read, besides being quite a bit of fun. —*Spirit of Change Magazine*

THE NEW PATH
My Life with Paramhansa Yogananda
Swami Kriyananda

The New Path is a moving revelation of one man's search for lasting happiness. After discarding the false promises offered by modern society, J. Donald Walters found himself (much to his surprise) at the feet of Paramhansa Yogananda, asking to become his disciple. How he got there, trained with the Master, and became Swami Kriyananda make fascinating reading.

The rest of the book is the only complete account of what it was like to live at the feet of that great man of God — one who was destined to bring major changes to the world.

Anyone hungering to learn more about Yogananda will delight in the hundreds of stories of life with a great avatar and the profound lessons they offer. This book is an ideal complement to *Autobiography of a Yogi.*

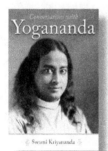

CONVERSATIONS WITH YOGANANDA
Recorded, with reflections, by his disciple,
Swami Kriyananda

For those who enjoyed Paramhansa Yogananda's autobiography and hunger for more, this collection of conversations offers rare intimate glimpses of life with the Master as never before shared.

This is an unparalleled account of Yogananda and his teachings written by one of his closest disciples. Swami Kriyananda was often present when Yogananda spoke privately with other close disciples, received visitors and answered their questions, and dictated and discussed his writings. He recorded the Master's words, preserving a treasure trove of wisdom that would otherwise have been lost.

These conversations include not only Yogananda's words as he spoke them but the added insight of a disciple who has spent over fifty years attuning his consciousness to that of his guru.

The collection features nearly five hundred stories, sayings, and insights from the twentieth century's most famous master of yoga, as well as twenty-five photos — almost all previously unreleased.

THE ESSENCE OF THE BHAGAVAD GITA
Explained by Paramhansa Yogananda
As remembered by his disciple, Swami Kriyananda

Rarely in a lifetime does a new spiritual classic appear that has the power to change people's lives and transform future generations. This is such a book. This revelation of India's best-loved scripture approaches it from a fresh perspective, showing its deep allegorical meaning and down-to-earth practicality. The themes presented are universal: how to achieve victory in life in union with the Divine; how to prepare for life's "final exam," death, and what happens afterward; and how to triumph over all pain and suffering.

The book itself is a triumph. Swami Kriyananda worked with Paramhansa Yogananda in 1950 while the Master completed his commentary. At that time, Yogananda commissioned him to disseminate his teachings worldwide.

"Millions will find God through this book!" Yogananda declared upon completion of the manuscript. *"Not just thousands — millions. I have seen it. I know."*

WHISPERS FROM ETERNITY
A Book of Answered Prayers
Paramhansa Yogananda
Edited by his disciple, Swami Kriyananda

Many poetic works can inspire, but few have the power to change lives. These poems and prayers carry extraordinary power, having been "spiritualized" by Paramhansa Yogananda: Each has drawn a response from the Divine. Yogananda was not only a master poet whose imagery here is still as vivid and alive as when first published in 1949: He was a spiritual master, an avatar.

He encouraged his disciples to read from *Whispers from Eternity* every day, explaining that through these verses he could guide them after his passing. But this book is not for his disciples alone. It is for spiritual aspirants of any tradition who wish to drink from this bountiful fountain of pure inspiration and wisdom.

~ THE WISDOM of YOGANANDA series ~

In this series, Yogananda offers timeless wisdom in an approachable, easy-to-read format. The writings of the Master are presented with minimal editing, to capture his expansive and compassionate wisdom, his sense of fun, and his practical spiritual guidance.

HOW TO BE HAPPY ALL THE TIME, volume 1

Yogananda explains everything needed to lead a happier, more fulfilling life: looking for happiness in the right places; choosing to be happy; tools, techniques, and methods for achieving happiness; sharing happiness with others; and balancing success with happiness.

KARMA AND REINCARNATION, volume 2

Yogananda reveals the reality of karma, death, reincarnation, and the afterlife. With clarity and simplicity, he makes the mysterious understandable: why we see a world of suffering and inequality; what happens at death and after death; the purpose of reincarnation; and how to handle the challenges we face in our lives.

HOW TO LOVE AND BE LOVED, volume 3

Practical guidance and fresh insight on relationships of all types are shared by Yogananda: how to cure friendship-ending habits; how to choose the right partner; the role of sex in marriage; how to conceive a spiritually oriented child; the solutions to problems that arise in marriage; and the Universal Love at the heart of all relationships.

HOW TO BE A SUCCESS, volume 4

The Attributes of Success, Yogananda's original booklet on reaching one's goals, is compiled with other writings on success: how to develop habits of success and eradicate habits of failure; thriving in the right job; how to build will power and magnetism; and finding the true purpose of one's life.

HOW TO HAVE COURAGE, CALMNESS, AND CONFIDENCE, volume 5

A master at helping people change and grow, Yogananda shows how to transform one's life: dislodge negative thoughts and depression; uproot fear and thoughts of failure; cure nervousness and systematically eliminate worry from life; and overcome anger, sorrow, oversensitivity, and a host of other troublesome emotions.

HOW TO ACHIEVE GLOWING HEALTH AND VITALITY, volume 6

Yogananda explains principles that promote physical health and overall well-being, mental clarity, and inspiration in one's spiritual life. He offers practical, wide-ranging, and fascinating suggestions on having more energy and living a radiantly healthy life. Readers will discover the priceless Energization Exercises for rejuvenating the body and mind, the fine art of conscious relaxation, and helpful diet tips for health and beauty.

HOW TO AWAKEN YOUR TRUE POTENTIAL, volume 7

With compassion, humor, and deep understanding of human psychology, Yogananda offers instruction on releasing limitations to access the power of mind and heart. Discover your hidden resources and be empowered to choose a life with greater meaning, purpose, and joy.

THE MAN WHO REFUSED HEAVEN, volume 8

Why is humor so deeply appreciated? Laughter is one of the great joys of life. Joy is fundamental to who we are. The humor in this book is taken from Yogananda's writings. Also included are experiences with the Master that demonstrate his playful spirit.

HOW TO FACE LIFE'S CHANGES, volume 9

Changes come not to destroy us, rather, to help us grow in understanding and to learn the lessons we must to reach our highest potential. Guided by Yogananda, tap into the changeless joy of your soul-nature, empowering you to move through life fearlessly and with an open heart. Learn to accept change as the reality of life; face change in relationships, finances, and health with gratitude; and cultivate key attitudes like fearlessness, non-attachment, and willpower.

HOW TO SPIRITUALIZE YOUR LIFE, volume 10
Yogananda answers a diverse range of questions asked by truth-seekers, sharing his teachings and insights on how to be successful in the everyday world and in one's spiritual life. Addressing financial, physical, mental, emotional, and spiritual challenges, he explains how best to expand one's consciousness and live life to the fullest. Compiled from his articles, lessons, and handwritten letters, this tenth volume in the Wisdom of Yogananda series was written in a question-and-answer format, well suited to both individual and group study.

HOW TO LIVE WITHOUT FEAR, volume 11
(Releases: March 2024)

More Selected Offerings from Crystal Clarity Publishers

Many of our titles are available in e-book and audiobook formats through our website and other popular online stores.

Demystifying Patanjali
The Wisdom of Paramhansa Yogananda
Presented by his direct disciple, Swami Kriyananda

Revelations of Christ
Proclaimed by Paramhansa Yogananda
Presented by his disciple, Swami Kriyananda

The Rubaiyat of Omar Khayyam Explained
Paramhansa Yogananda
Edited by his disciple, Swami Kriyananda

For Starters series
Meditation *by Swami Kriyananda*
Intuition *by Swami Kriyananda*
Chakras *by Savitri Simpson*
Vegetarian Cooking *by Diksha McCord*

Secrets series
Swami Kriyananda
Meditation and Inner Peace • Success and Leadership
Health and Healing • Spiritualizing Your Daily Life

Touch of Light series
Nayaswami Jyotish and Nayaswami Devi Novak
Touch of Light • Touch of Joy
Touch of Love • Touch of Peace
Touch of Divine Wisdom *(release: July 2023)*

Affirmations for Self-Healing
Swami Kriyananda

AUM: The Melody of Love
Joseph Bharat Cornell

Divine Will Healing
Mary Kretzmann

Eastern Thoughts, Western Thoughts
Swami Kriyananda

The Essential Flower Essence Handbook
Lila Devi

The Flawless Mirror
Kamala Silva

Flow Learning
Joseph Bharat Cornell

The Four Stages of Yoga
Nischala Cryer

God Is for Everyone
Inspired by Paramhansa Yogananda
As taught to and understood by his disciple, Swami Kriyananda

The Harmonium Handbook
Satyaki Kraig Brockschmidt

The Hindu Way of Awakening
Swami Kriyananda

How to Meditate
Jyotish Novak

Loved and Protected
Asha Nayaswami

The Meaning of Dreaming
Savitri Simpson

My Heart Remembers
Narayani Anaya

The Need for Spiritual Communities
Swami Kriyananda

A Pilgrimage to Guadalupe
Swami Kriyananda

The Promise of Immortality
Swami Kriyananda

Sharing Nature
Joseph Bharat Cornell

Solving Stress
Kraig Brockschmidt

Spiritual Yoga
Gyandev McCord

Stand Unshaken!
Nayaswamis Jyotish and Devi

Swami Kriyananda As We Have Known Him
Asha (Praver) Nayaswami

Swamiji
Miriam Rodgers

Transitioning in Grace
Nalini Graeber

Two Souls: Four Lives
Catherine Kairavi

The Yoga of Abraham Lincoln
Richard Salva

Your Sun Sign as a Spiritual Guide
Swami Kriyananda

The Yugas
Joseph Selbie and David Steinmetz

CPSIA information can be obtained
at www.ICGtesting.com
Printed in the USA
JSHW020805170323
39064JS00004B/17